STUDIES IN MANAGEMENT

EDITED BY

ANDREW ROBERTSON

*National Institute of Economic
and Social Research*

No. 1

BUSINESS ORGANIZATION

Studies in Management

2. CORPORATE PLANNING
   by John Argenti

3. THE MANAGER'S GUIDE TO INDUSTRIAL RELATIONS
   by L. F. Neal and Andrew Robertson

4. THE NUMERATE MANAGER
   by F. Keay

5. BRITISH MANAGEMENT THOUGHT
   by John Child

6. STAFF REPORTING AND STAFF DEVELOPMENT
   by Edgar Anstey

7. MANAGERIAL AND PROFESSIONAL STAFF GRADING
   by Joan Doulton and David Hay

8. OWNERSHIP, CONTROL AND IDEOLOGY
   by Theo Nichols

JOHN O'SHAUGHNESSY

Associate Professor in Business, Graduate School of Business, Columbia University, New York.

BUSINESS ORGANIZATION

London

GEORGE ALLEN & UNWIN LTD

RUSKIN HOUSE · MUSEUM STREET

FIRST PUBLISHED IN 1966
SECOND IMPRESSION WITH CORRECTIONS 1968
THIRD IMPRESSION WITH CORRECTIONS 1969
FOURTH IMPRESSION 1971
FIFTH IMPRESSION 1973

© *George Allen & Unwin Ltd.*, 1966
ISBN 0 04 658008 5 hardback
ISBN 0 04 658043 3 paperback

PRINTED IN GREAT BRITAIN BY
COMPTON PRINTING LTD
LONDON AND AYLESBURY

FOREWORD

If business executives already have too much to read, what can be the justification for offering them still more? One answer to this compelling question is that this series has been so designed that it should help the busy manager to short circuit the literature and still arrive at a developed and informed stage of self improvement, assuming that he believes that such a course is necessary.

There have been numerous books published on general management principles and practice, and the repetition from one book to the next has, not unnaturally, been considerable. At the same time, each book of any merit has carried management understanding a step further. In this series the aim has been to place before the management student (and he need not necessarily be undergoing a formal course of study) a profile of management thought and practice in the past half century, during which economic thinking has matured and management theorising has been trying out its first few stumbling paces.

For historical reasons there has been much more activity in management studies in the United States than in Europe, and consequently the literature, especially for the English speaking countries, has been dominated by American writers. A great deal of what they have had to offer has been of immense value, but nevertheless the approach has not always been appropriate to the British industrial and commercial scene. In recent years, therefore, British managers have welcomed the emergence of a management literature in their own country, which is more directly suited to their needs, and it is the hope and expectation of the editor and authors of this series that it will take its place alongside the existing material, and supplement it in a useful way.

Each contribution to the Studies in Management series is planned to be comprehensive and analytical, surveying the particular field of study, commenting helpfully upon it and, where possible, offering dispassionate judgements. As far as management studies can be comprehended in separate compartments these books will attempt, to initiate the newcomer and refresh the veteran, beginning with organization theory, which has had a complex and involved development, moving on to management principles and their application, to industrial sociology, industrial relations and other well defined areas of study.

At this juncture in the shaping of management studies, textbooks intended to provide short cuts for the examinee may not be merely premature but positively misleading. It has been assumed that what is most needed is a reasonably brief, readable, and reliable account of what has been written, said or done, and to what point this thought and application has brought the practising manager on his long road to 'professionalism'.

Management studies is not at a crossroads. In its present state it is more apt to say that it has reached a roundabout off which there are many roads. Perhaps this series can supply a few fingerposts.

ANDREW ROBERTSON

BUSINESS organization theory is expanding rapidly, so much so that even the professional student of the subject finds difficulty in keeping abreast of the literature. There are different schools of thought, which in this book are broadly grouped into the classical, the human relations and the systems, and which speak different languages, take different viewpoints and are often antagonistic towards each other. How then is the businessman, with so little time to spare, to avoid the bewilderment which arises from the conflicting advice offered to him?

This book reviews the various approaches and mediates between the hostile points of view. Only the three approaches defined above are still distinguished. Each of these could, however, have been broken down still further as this broad classification ignores many minor differences among writers that could give rise to sub-grouping and cross-grouping.

The aim of this book is to give the reader an understanding of the many factors that appear relevant to a study of business organization. The view expressed is that these factors should be drawn from all three approaches; no one approach has a mono-poly of relevant theory. It is not intended to be encyclopaedic, but rather to give a broad survey in which the emphasis is on the more immediately useful branches of the theory.

Throughout the book, theoretical findings are supplemented by examples drawn from the practical problems of business manage-ment. Not only do they cover production and administration, but many of them are also drawn from the field of marketing. The inclusion of these latter is deliberate, since so many textbooks on organization have neglected this important function.

The structure of the book, the selection of its topics and the opinions expressed in it are the responsibility of the author alone. Nevertheless, it could not have been written without the help of colleagues, both in business and the academic field. Prominent among these are Professor T. Singleton, R. Stansfield, P. A. Losty, R. G. Lacey and Professor F. de P. Hanika. Special mention must be made of the contribution made by Professor S. Eilon and M. B. Godfrey in reading the drafts in detail and making suggestions for their improvement.

In preparing this book I have also had the able assistance of my Cranfield colleague, Albert Battersby, who more than anyone helped in the preparation of the manuscript and editing and revising my drafts. My thanks are also due to the 'ghost squad'— Ann Smith who typed the manuscript, Johnny Johnson who helped to prepare the illustrations and my wife who acted as my amanuensis.

Finally, I am grateful to the following for permission to reproduce diagrams from their publications:

Richard D. Irwin, Tavistock Publications, Holt, Rinehart & Winston, Inc., Management International, University of Illinois Press, McGraw-Hill Book Company and John Wiley and Sons.

CONTENTS

FOREWORD   page   7

PREFACE   9

I. INTRODUCTION   13
*Approaches to organization—Setting objectives—Time span covered by
objectives—Coverage—Primary objective, profit—Secondary objectives:
marketing, product innovation, efficiency—Departmental objectives—
Difficulties in setting objectives.*

II. THE CLASSICAL APPROACH   26
*Determining objectives—Grouping activities—Span of control—
Grouping to achieve economies of scale—Grouping to achieve co-ordination—Grouping by nature of activity—Conflict of factors—Co-ordination and committees—Co-ordination and divisionalization—Delegating
authority—Decentralization and Divisionalization—Specifying responsibility or accountability for performance—Establishing relationships—
Work organization.*

III. THE HUMAN RELATIONS APPROACH   72
*Individual needs and wants—Behaviour of work groups—Behaviour of
the supervisor—Inter-group behaviour—Human relations and classical
organization problems.*

IV. THE SYSTEMS APPROACH   125
*Systems definition—Systems approach to organization—Specifying
objectives—Listing the sub-systems, or main decision areas—Analysing
the decision areas and establishing information needs—Designing the
communication channels for the information flow—Grouping decision
areas to minimize communications burden—The systems contribution
to classical organization problems.*

POSTSCRIPT AND SUMMARY   162

APPENDIX I. ILLUSTRATIVE SYSTEMS STUDY   170
          II. DECISION SCHEDULE   187

REFERENCES   192

INDEX   197

CHAPTER 1

INTRODUCTION

APPROACHES TO ORGANIZATION

If the work of running a business is beyond the capacity of one person to perform, it has to be shared out among others. This brings with it the problem of getting people to act in unison with each other. Organization is a matter of dividing work among people whose efforts will have to be co-ordinated. In practice, it is also concerned with specifying objectives for the business as a whole and each of its sub-units and determining, in broad terms, the activities and decisions necessary to accomplish these objectives.

Deficiencies in organization give rise to many inefficiencies:

(i) Departments and sections may be unable to contribute sufficient to overall objectives to justify their cost. Conversely, objectives may be pursued unsatisfactorily because of a reluctance to set up a section or department (for example a costing or market research department), the existence of which is a prerequisite to achieving adequate end results.

(ii) Functions may not be co-ordinated on a companywide basis. For example, a uniform policy on recruitment or wages may be lacking, its absence leading to anomalies and conflict between departments.

(iii) There may be a failure to co-ordinate interdepartmental activities. As a consequence, overall economies may be sacrificed and 'bottlenecks' in the flow of work may arise as each department acts independently of others.

(iv) Decisions may be too slow and poor in quality because (a) the managers concerned are overloaded, (b) the information required for decision-making is not readily available, or (c) the decisions are being made at the wrong place or level.

Three main approaches to organization can be distinguished: **Classical, Human Relations** and **Systems**. All three approaches cover aspects of organization which cannot be ignored though they emphasize factors that sometimes pull in opposite directions. Fig. 1 illustrates each of the approaches.

The classical approach to organization is to study the *activities* that need to be undertaken to achieve objectives. Once these activities are identified, they are grouped to form individual jobs, sections and higher administrative units, the aim being to get efficient specialization and co-ordination without physically overloading supervisors or managers. Co-ordination is further facilitated by linking people together in a chain of command and by ensuring that each person knows where his responsibilities end and another's begins. The classical approach also attempts to establish rules (the so-called 'principles' of organization) to act as criteria in developing an organization.

The human relations approach starts with a study of man's *motives* and *behaviour*. From such a study, criteria are derived which will help in designing an organization that stimulates people to co-operate in achieving the aims of the business. There can be no effective co-ordination of activities unless people are willing to co-operate, and such co-operation is not achieved automatically but may be evoked by the organization.

The systems approach concentrates on the *decisions* that need to be made to achieve objectives; the organization is thus designed to facilitate decision-making. Decision-making, rather than activities, is chosen for study because it is through the process of decision-making that policies are laid down and actions taken that result in the future success of the company. However, since decisions require information and information has to be communicated, the approach not only studies the decision process itself but also the information and communication which precede and succeed it. Communication of information is vital in the large business, as without it there can be neither co-operation nor co-ordination.

SETTING OBJECTIVES

A company seeks certain objectives: each activity within a company derives its significance from the contribution it makes to them. If we were to seek improvement of an organization

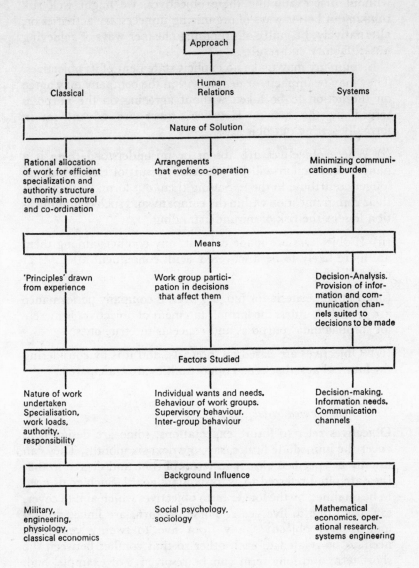

	Approach	
Classical	Human Relations	Systems

Nature of Solution

Rational allocation of work for efficient specialization and authority structure to maintain control and co-ordination	Arrangements that evoke co-operation	Minimizing communications burden

Means

'Principles' drawn from experience	Work group participation in decisions that affect them	Decision-Analysis. Provision of information and communication channels suited to decisions to be made

Factors Studied

Nature of work undertaken Specialisation, work loads, authority, responsibility	Individual wants and needs. Behaviour of work groups. Supervisory behaviour. Inter-group behaviour	Decision-making. Information needs. Communication channels

Background Influence

Military, engineering, physiology, classical economics	Social psychology, sociology	Mathematical economics, operational research, systems engineering

Fig. 1.—Organization.

without first examining these objectives, we might well risk
thinking of better ways of organizing unnecessary activities or,
alternatively, be guilty of proposing cheaper ways of achieving
unsatisfactory end-results.

A company may make no explicit statement of its objectives.
They may be implicit, or people within the company may agree
on the action to be taken without agreeing on the purposes
served by the action. However, there are advantages in
formally setting out objectives.

(i) Where objectives are absent or misunderstood there is a
danger that action will be taken in pursuit of ends which no
longer contribute to them. Setting them out formally facilitates
their communication within the company and such communication lessens the risk of misunderstanding.

(ii) If objectives are made explicit, any conflicts among them
are more likely to be discovered, with consequent attempts at
reconciliation.

(iii) Explicit criteria for judging overall company performance
are provided, unless the formal statement of objectives is merely
for 'propaganda' purposes and conceals the true ones.

(iv) Objectives are based on forecasts, and it is by considering
the future that setbacks and opportunities are anticipated.

Time Span Covered by Objectives

Objectives refer to future expectations; some are designed to
cover the immediate future, say, the next six months. They can
usually be specified clearly in terms of time and degree so that
they are often referred to as 'proximate goals'. Such goals need
to be qualified by the longer term objectives which aim to cover,
say, from one to five years. These, in turn, are linked to still
longer term objectives, say from five to twenty years. All
need to be related to each other so that conflict between the
short term and long term can be resolved. For example, high
profit may be achieved during the short period by lowering
quality, but this may be at the expense of the longterm profit
position.

Objectives are based on assumptions about the future. Hence
their reliability depends on the extent to which future con-

ditions can be forecast. The further ahead the period considered, the greater the uncertainty about the future and the more the objectives have to be stated in general terms.

This chapter is mainly concerned with setting objectives for the one-to-five year period; no single orderly sequence of steps exists for doing so. There is a large element of trial and error since each step taken depends on information derived from other steps.

Coverage

Objectives are set in series. In Fig. 2, each tread on the staircase symbolizes an objective and each riser symbolizes a means. Any

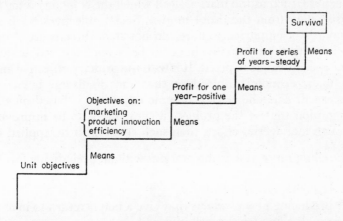

FIG. 2.—Each tread of the staircase symbolizes an objective and each riser symbolizes a means. Each objective is thus an intermediate goal serving as a means of achieving some higher objective.

objective can thus be shown to be an intermediate goal serving as a means in achieving some higher objective. If we are justified in speaking of *ultimate* objectives, that of a company is to survive; this, in turn, necessitates making a steady profit. However, to declare survival to be the objective of a company would be too broad a guide line for organization planning. We need to descend the staircase and declare how survival is to be sought. Here information is needed about economic, techno-logical, social and political trends, and company resources and existing commitments must be assessed. On the basis of such data, objectives are chosen. They can be classified as in the diagram below

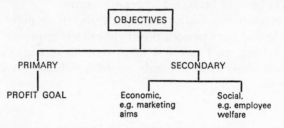

The *primary* objective is to make a steady profit. Secondary objectives can be either economic or social. Economic objectives, such as the market need which the company aims to satisfy, stem from the profit motive. Social objectives, such as standards of employee welfare, do not stem directly from the profit motive but usually have to be accommodated within some specific range of profit. It is with the primary objective and the main economic objectives that the discussion below is concerned. The choice of economic objectives is based on the recognition that, if the profit of a company is to be improved through managerial effort, then such effort must be applied to

(i)   selling more at existing margins without prejudicing future sales,
(ii)   reducing costs,
(iii) producing new products that give a better return to investment allowing for the risk involved.

Primary Objective—Profit

Profit is the primary objective of any company in a free enterprise economy. It is sometimes denied that this is so and that other goals may be equal or more important. Chamberlain, an economist, points out that top company executives have contributed to this belief by claiming multiple responsibilities—not only to shareholders but to the community, suppliers, employees, customers, and acknowledging that the interests of all these parties are not equally served by the pursuit of profit.[1] However, top executives seldom explain a low profit position by acknowledging the priority of other goals except when these other goals have been forced upon them, as when BOAC claimed that its losses arose mainly from being compelled by the Government to stake millions of pounds 'unseen' on new British aircraft, and to being required to run services ('carry the flag') along unprofitable routes.

Directors of a public company do not enjoy an easy life if they make relatively low profits. They are subject to criticism from financial commentators since profit is the criterion used in assessing whether the effort put into producing and selling is worth more than the expense of doing so. They may also have difficulty in raising capital; additionally they run the risk of a take-over and finding themselves jobless. In any case, progress in many companies is almost 'institutionalized'.

Units are set up whose sole function is to improve the profit position of the company and budgeting procedures are established which emphasize cost reduction and profit. Profit may thus become the primary objective even if top management regard profit as merely one among a number of equally important objectives.

It is not suggested that companies seek singlemindedly *maximum* profit as theoretical economists assume, but that they seek first and foremost to achieve a 'satisfactory' profit. Where several objectives are considered primary ones (as has been the case with our nationalized industries) emphasis on objectives may vary more in tune with the politics of the moment than with changes in the market or technology. One single unambiguous criterion, such as profit, simplifies the search for and the selection of relevant means, as it is a basis for choice.

If profit is the primary objective, what constitutes a satisfactory profit? There are many difficulties in making the concept of profit operational. Although a company in the long run aims at a steady rate of return that justifies the risk undertaken, the interpretation of the terms used in this statement require many judgments to be made, namely,

(i)   'In the long run.' How far in the future are profits to be calculated?

(ii) 'Rate of return.' Is the rate of return to be calculated on sales, net worth or total assets?

(iii) 'Risks undertaken.' How are we to combine profits and probabilities in making a choice? A company which is short of capital might prefer a 10 per cent return to invest-

ment that is certain rather than a 50 per cent return with
a 10 per cent probability of making a loss.

A discussion of these problems is beyond the scope of this
book, though they are frequently debated.[2, 3]

Secondary Objectives—Marketing

The major secondary objective generally relates to marketing.
Marketing considerations enter into all decisions within the
company. For example, investment decisions deal with the
kinds of facilities needed to supply future consumer needs; those
concerned with recruitment and training must consider the
tasks that consumer needs will impose on the business. Hence
company objectives should normally embrace a marketing
objective to guide such decision making.

Market specialists generally recommend that a firm should
state first the generic need for which it caters before setting out
the specific need. For example, a watch manufacturer might
state that he caters for the need to measure time though his
specific market segment is the need for a compact, easy to carry,
instrument for measuring time.[4]

The reasons for first stating the generic need are twofold.

1. It defines the firm's main competition; Peter Drucker argues
that the gas cooker manufacturer should consider his business
as that of supplying an easy way to cook, so that he recognizes
that his competition will come from all suppliers of acceptable
ways of cooking food.[5] It has also been pointed out that, if
Hollywood had considered first and foremost that it was in
the mass entertainment business rather than merely films, it
would have been in a better position to anticipate the competition from television.

2. A second reason for stating the generic need is to avoid
commitment to a market segment without first considering the
wider range of possibilities available. The number of solutions
to a problem 'increases with the generality and broadness of the
problem statement and decreases with the number of restrictions and inhibiting words in the statement.'[6] A firm that considers first that it is in the business to satisfy the need to *get rid
of rats* will initially consider a wider range of alternatives than
the firm that decides it is in business to satisfy the need *to kill
rats*.

Overall objectives should also state the specific market segment that the company seek to exploit as it is this particular segment need that will most influence decision making within the company. For example, an article in *Business Week* points out that at the Remington Arms Company, the management believes the customer to be primarily interested in the 'best possible product at the lowest possible cost' but that, on the other hand the Winchester Western Company follows the theory that 'the shooter doesn't buy a gun like a tool. It wraps up romance and pride of possession, the "Cadillac idea", with every gun.' In the first company everything is geared to simplicity, speed, efficiency and mass production; in the second everything is geared to craft, quality and custom touches, even at an extra price. The article notes that both ideas work. However, management decision making in the two companies will take place within different frames of reference.[7]

Secondary Objectives—Product Innovation and Development

The long-term prosperity of a company may depend on bringing out a constant stream of new products or services, as is the case in the electronics industry today. Existing products may only have a brief life-cycle and product innovation is necessary to enable the company to maintain its profit level or, additionally, is the main means open to the company for expansion.

The development of new products involves all the major functions of a company—marketing, finance, purchasing, manufacturing, etc. When company objectives include a statement of aims about product innovation, managers are prepared for what the change involves, given help in understanding the purpose of newly created specialist posts and made to feel that the company is progressive. All these must exist throughout the firm if everyone is to co-operate with those concerned in co-ordinating the activities on which the product innovation and development depend.

Economic Objectives—Efficiency

If the profit goal is to be achieved, efficiency needs to be encouraged. Efficiency may be distinguished from effectiveness. Effectiveness is the extent to which the task undertaken is achieved, whereas efficiency is the extent to which the task is achieved relative to the cost. To increase efficiency may require that problems (such as inventory control or order handling procedures) be looked at interdepartmentally. Such work is often carried out by central specialist staff acting at the request of top management. It is advisable for overall company objectives to set out explicitly the declared aims of any programme for improving efficiency. For example, the declared aim might be to reduce the cost of interdepartmental clerical procedures by 15 per cent within two years. In this way the purpose of certain central services is made known and their job facilitated.

Objectives at Departmental Level

Objectives can be set for each department of the company to ensure that departmental goals are consistent with overall objectives. Departmental objectives can be further divided into goals for each departmental sub-unit to carry goal-focused planning well down the line. For example, the overall marketing objective might lay down the level of sales and the percentage share of the market that ought to be achieved at a specified total marketing cost. This presupposes (among other things) that a certain number of consumers have gone through the stages of being aware of the company's product, developing a favourable attitude towards it and finally preferring it to competitive makes.

In such circumstances the goals for advertising might be laid down as illustrated in the table opposite. Information on existing consumer awareness (stage 1) may be obtained through market research and a distinction made on the basis of whether or not the consumer was helped to recall the product. Similarly, information through market research can be obtained on whether the consumer comprehended the advertising message (stage 2), or the degree to which he is favourably disposed towards the product (stage 3), and his buying habits (stage 4). The target goals (column 2) are laid down after considering the cost of achieving various goal levels.

Difficulties in Setting Objectives

The discussion so far has tended to oversimplify the problem of setting objectives. There are many difficulties. One of them, already mentioned, is that of making profit into an operational concept. Objectives should preferably be stated in quantitative terms but this is not always possible. However, merely to specify a healthy future existence to be an objective is too vague for control purposes; something more specific is demanded.

Stages	Existing % (1)	Goal % (2)	Actual % (3)	Variance % (4)
1. *Awareness of Product 'A'*				
Unaided recall of product	15	30		
Aided recall of product	35	65		
2. *Comprehend Message*				
Message 'X'	10	25		
Message 'Y'	20	45		
3. *Favourably Disposed*				
To product 'A'	5	11		
4. *Bought Once*				
For reasons given in message	1	3		
For other reasons	1	1		
Bought Regularly				
For reasons given in message	2	5		
For other reasons	2	2		

Objectives may often conflict. Ideally, relative weights should be attached to the various objectives so that they may be combined into a single index indicating overall performance. For example:

Objectives	Weight	% Achievement	Weight × Achievement
A	10	75	750
B	3	90	270
C	4	105	420
D	1	110	110
E	2	70	140
Total	20		Total 1,690

$$\therefore \text{ Index of Performance } \frac{1,690}{20} = 84.5.$$

In practice there appears to be a large element of bargaining when objectives are set. A firm during its history has accepted commitments which cannot now be ignored and concessions have to be made to various people connected with the organization to get them to co-operate and submerge their differences. Bargains made in the past set precedents, such as a policy on redundancy, and may limit the choice of objectives in the future. In fact, objectives may be so firmly determined by a successive series of such partial commitments that the manager has no room for manœuvre. Sometimes, too, the management hesitate to specify objectives or else state them in vague terms in order to avoid conflict. Inconsistencies between objectives are often ignored, in that each is examined in turn rather than all of them together.

There is a danger in setting objectives in such specific detail that they become too restrictive, objectives being prescribed to managers at a lower level without their participation and without making use of their specific technical 'know-how'. Battersby in the field of network analysis comments as follows:

'no work should be detailed to such an extent that the supervisor has no freedom to make adjustments on the spot. He should not be "programmed out of his job". This may apply just as strongly to higher management: some American contractors have resented over-networking by Government offices, with its implied intrusion into their own administration.'[8]

It might be useful at this stage to make a distinction between objectives and policies. Objectives emphasize aims and are stated as expectations, but policies emphasize rules and are stated in the form of directives. For example:

Marketing	Objective:	complete market coverage
	Policy:	the Company *will* sell to every retail outlet that is creditworthy, as decided by the Company Accountant.
Production	Objective:	low unit costs from long production runs
	Policy:	the Company *will not* produce one-off jobs without the specific authority of the Board.
Finance	Objective:	to maintain adequate liquidity
	Policy:	accountant will draw up a cash budget and inform the Board if working capital is likely to fall below a specified limit.

Personnel Objective: good labour relations
Policy: Set up and maintain schemes for: Joint Consultation, Job Evaluation, Wage Incentives.

There may be financial difficulties, as well as psychological and technical ones, in achieving objectives. The main financial test occurs during the budgeting process which translates objectives into financial terms. Company budgeting starts with a forecast of sales which, if acceptable, forms the basis for the sales budget from which stem all other budgets. All budgets are finally subsumed into the projected balance sheet. Wherever an unsatisfactory financial position is revealed by the main projected budgets—balance sheet, profit and loss, capital and cash —the objectives may need to be modified in order to achieve the profit goal.

CHAPTER II

THE CLASSICAL APPROACH

THE classical approach was the first to develop. It is associated with the writings of Fayol (1916) in France, Taylor (1911), Mooney and Reilly (1932) in America, Urwick (1928, 1943) in Britain, and, more recently, with the writings of Brech (1957) in Britain and Allen (1958) in America. These writers have contributed most to the approach. All have been managers or management consultants.

Although it is now fashionable in management literature to portray the approach as out of date, this opinion is very much open to question. It is included in this book because it focuses attention on factors which cannot be ignored in any study on organization. The approach concentrates on the following problems:

1. Determining objectives and deducing from these broad objectives a more detailed specification of the work to be done.

2. Grouping activities into sections, then sections into departments and higher administrative units.

3. Delegating authority.

4. Specifying responsibility or accountability for performance.

5. Establishing formal relationships among employees so that each knows his position in the team.

Although classical writers have made the above problems their chief concern, one further problem might be added to complete the list.

6. Organizing work at shop floor level.

DETERMINING OBJECTIVES AND
DEDUCING FROM THESE BROAD OBJECTIVES
A MORE DETAILED SPECIFICATION OF
THE WORK TO BE DONE

Rice of the Tavistock Institute claims 'Classical organizational models are for the most part based on closed systems. The implicit assumption is made that the organizational problems of an enterprise can be analysed by reference only to its internal environment and that any change in the external environment can be accommodated within the existing organization.[9]'

Other writers have commented similarly. Such criticism might leave the impression that the classical approach ignores the external environment. This view can hardly be reconciled with the facts. Urwick argues:

'Forecasting has its own principle, namely, Appropriateness. It enters into process with Organization, since the first thing you do when you look ahead is to try to provide the means, human and material, to meet the future situation which you foresee. Its effect is Co-ordination.'[10]

'It is impossible to plan in a void, about nothing; the conception of making a plan postulates that it is a plan to do something. There must be an objective.'[11]

Urwick defines 'appropriateness' as seeing 'that the human and material organization are suitable for the objects, resources and needs of the undertaking'. Henri Fayol, the most famous classical writer on management, was also aware of the relationship between the external environment and organization. He argued that a company must have a plan of action which rests

'(1) on the firm's resources (buildings, tools, raw materials, personnel, productive capacity, sales outlets, public relations, etc.),
(2) on the nature and importance of work in progress,
(3) on future trends which depend partly on technical, commercial, financial and other conditions, all subject to change, whose importance and occurrence cannot be predetermined.'[12]

He later goes on to say that 'the organization has to carry out the following managerial duties:

'(1) ensure that the plan is judiciously prepared and strictly carried out,

(2) see that the human and material organization is consistent with the objectives, resources and requirements of the concern.'[13]

These quotations are from a chapter entitled 'Elements of Management' in Fayol's *General and Industrial Management*. The whole chapter is evidence that Fayol saw the importance of setting objectives and their relevance to organization.

In recent years the classical approach has shown an increasing emphasis on setting objectives as a prerequisite to any organization work. Urwick, for example, stresses the necessity of detailing objectives to determine whether all existing activities justify their existence and whether additional activities might profitably be undertaken.

'The organization should only exist in order to carry out some specific purpose implicit in the forecast and the plan. Every piece of it should make a definite and authorized contribution to that purpose. Otherwise there is no reason for its existence.'[14]

There is, of course, a practical difficulty in assessing the contribution of some activities. Thus, Simon of the Carnegie Institute of Technology comments:

'Most organizations are oriented around some goal or objective which provides the purpose toward which the organization decisions and activities are directed. If the goal is relatively tangible—making shoes for example—it is usually not too difficult to assess the contribution of specific activities toward it, and hence to evaluate their usefulness. If the goal is less tangible—like that of a religious organization—it becomes more debatable whether a particular activity contributes to the goal; and hence there may be considerable controversy, even among those who wish to work for the goal, as to how it is to be attained. Even where the goal is tangible there may be some activities whose relation to it is so indirect, though not necessarily any less substantial for that indirectness, that the problem of evaluation is difficult. It is much easier to budget, for example, for the production line than for the advertising department or for supervision.'[15]

Several writers, including Allen, point out that establishing objectives helps to determine management priorities. In particular, 'key' departments and activities can be identified. In some industries, for example, a firm's survival is impossible unless products are replaced before they become obsolete. In this situation a 'key' department would be product planning, including research and development, since its efficient functioning would be vital to the attainment of objectives. Such key departments demand key attention. Other departments exist to serve them. Experience suggests that where key departments are not formally identified, the attention of top management is focused on to minor issues raised by forceful managers—the 'decibel' system of management. In a dynamic situation some departments will lose their key position. This should be recognized and priorities adjusted. Failure to make adjustment dissipates managerial effort. For example, finance may be key during the growth of a business when an expanding market needs capital to finance growth. As the company acquires large financial reserves, the continued predominance of finance may unduly restrict imaginative marketing ventures.

GROUPING INTO SECTIONS, DEPARTMENTS AND HIGHER ADMINISTRATIVE UNITS

A section can be defined as a group of workers under one supervisor. Sections are grouped to form larger administrative units. The problem is to determine the basis for grouping people into sections and sections into departments and higher administrative units. Why, for example, should 'K' in Fig. 3 be grouped under 'G' rather than 'F' or 'E'?

The classical approach distinguishes four factors relevant to the problem:

1. *Span of control.* Grouping must ensure that each supervisor and manager is not overburdened with subordinates. This is described as the span of control.

2. *Economies of scale.* Grouping together similar activities may result in economies arising from larger scale production. Grouping should seek to achieve these economies.

3. *Co-ordination.* Grouping must ensure the co-ordination of activities and, other things remaining equal, the particular grouping chosen should minimize co-ordination problems.

4. *Nature of activity*. The nature of the activity should influence the level at which grouping takes place. 'Key' activities, for example, demand high-level attention and may need to be grouped directly under higher management.

The above factors may conflict with each other; for instance a grouping that improves co-ordination may conflict with one that leads to maximum economies arising from increasing the scale of operations.

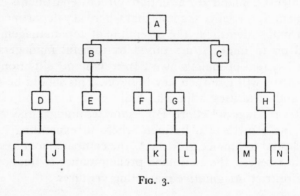

FIG. 3.

SPAN OF CONTROL

Both Fayol and Urwick have advocated a strict upper limit to the number of subordinates reporting to any one executive. Urwick, a British management consultant, argues that 'the ideal number of subordinates for all superior authorities . . . to be four' . . . however, 'at the lowest level of organization where what is delegated is responsibility for the performance of specific tasks and not for the supervision of others, the number may be eight or twelve'.[16] This has come to be known as the span of control principle.

A fixed span of control has many advocates in military history. Even Genghis Khan organized his hunters and herdsmen in such a way that every ten men were under a 'leader of ten' and every ten 'leaders of ten' were put under a 'leader of a hundred' and every ten 'leaders of a hundred' were put under a 'leader of a thousand'. However, Genghis Khan himself had at one time ninety-three 'leaders of a thousand' under his command!

The span of control problem receives a great deal of attention in classical management literature on the ground that the manager must be given time to co-ordinate and control the work of those under him. Graicunas, a French mathematician and consultant, argued that the limiting factor in the span of control is the number of *relationships* supervised and not merely the number of jobs and people supervised. In a paper published in 1933, Graicunas distinguished three subordinate-superior relationships that occur when the work of subordinates is inter-related.[17]

(1) The direct single relationship is the direct relationship between subordinate and superior. Hence the number of direct single relationships is equal to the number of subordinates supervised. In the simplest case, if A, the supervisor, has two subordinates, X and Y, there are two direct single relationships.

A with X
A with Y

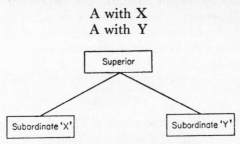

FIG. 4.—Direct single relationship.

(2) Cross-relationships are those arising from subordinates of a common superior having to consult one another. If the number of subordinates reporting to a common superior is N then the number of cross-relationships would be $N(N-1)$. For example, if A has subordinates, X and Y, the cross-relationships would be

X to Y
Y to X

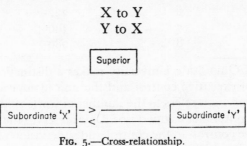

FIG. 5.—Cross-relationship.

(3) Direct group relationships are those between the superior and each possible combination of subordinates. For example,

where A has subordinates X and Y the direct group relationships would be

A and X with Y present
A and Y with X present

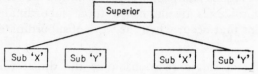

Fig. 6.—Direct group relationship.

Graicunas claimed that all the above relationships could potentially make demands on the supervisor's time. Even the cross-relationship might require the supervisor to act as mediator. However, where the work of subordinates is not interrelated, there is no need to consider either cross or direct group relationships. Graicunas expressed the total number of relationships as

$$N\left(\frac{2^N}{2}+N-1\right)$$

where N = Number of subordinates. This gives for example:

No. of subordinates	Total relationships
1	1
2 . . .	6
3	18
4	44
5	100
6	222
7	490
8	1,080

Davis of Ohio State University makes a distinction between the span of executive control and the unit of supervision. The unit of supervision refers to the number of workers at shop floor level to be put under a supervisor. Davis reserves the term 'span of executive control' to the control and supervision of managers and supervisors. He justifies this distinction on the ground that the problems at shop floor level are much simpler than those at managerial level. Because of this the relationships between supervisor and worker are less demanding. Davis claims the unit of supervision can range from ten to thirty employees, whereas the optimum span of executive control is generally around five people.[18]

Criticism of Span of Control Principle

Spans v. Number of Levels. Simon of the Carnegie Institute of Technology points out that 'a limited span of control is in conflict with the principle that the number of levels in an organization should be kept to as few as is practically possible.' He argues that 'if you increase the span of control, you decrease the number of levels, and if you decrease the span of control you increase the number of levels . . . . For an organization of 6,500 members, an average span of control of three will call for 9 levels ($3^8 = 6,561$ and one extra level for top executive); an average span of control of 9 will call for 5 levels ($9^4 = 6,561$). This means that the price of reducing the span of control is always some increase in the number of levels; the price of reducing the number of levels is some increase in the span of control.'[19]

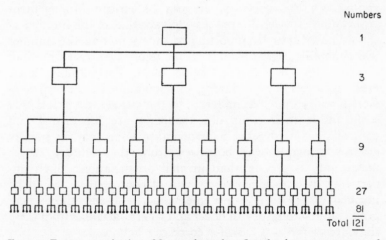

FIG. 7.—For an organization of 81 people at shop floor level an average span of control of 3 calls for five levels and 40 additional staff at supervisory and management level.

Simon can be misleading if it is not borne in mind that the 6,500 members are at non-supervisory level. The eight levels above them will contain a further 3,280 supervisory staff in all,

c

so the *total* organization will contain 9,841 people—half as many again. This point is illustrated by Fig. 7 in which once again the supervisory staff add an extra 50 per cent. If the span of control is nine, the total supervisory staff is only 820. In general, the ratio of supervisory to non-supervisory staff diminishes as the span of control increases. This is important since the span of control does appear to increase as a firm grows in size. Thus in a group of firms studied by Haire[20] those having between twenty and fifty employees had an average span of control of 11·5 subordinates per superior. However, when these firms grew to a size of more than 200 employees, the average span of control increased to twenty-one, and the percentage of employees in top and middle management dropped from 13·6 per cent to 4·1 per cent.

Span Varies with Situation. Other writers have argued similarly to Simon; although reducing 'spans' tends to improve horizontal communication, it also tends to affect adversely the vertical levels of communication as more levels are added. Suojanen of the University of California makes a number of additional criticisms. He claims there is no evidence for a fixed span of control. On the contrary, an AMA (American Management Association) survey showed a wide variation in the number of subordinates actually reporting to superiors, and the number was generally greater than four, the figure mentioned by both Urwick and Graicunas as being ideal. Furthermore, since executives spend time outside their companies, their span of work is wider than that indicated by the AMA survey, as it is only while inside their companies that they are supervising and controlling subordinates. Suojanen also claims that the span of control principle was borrowed from the military where uncertainty is greater than in civil organizations. Such uncertainty dictates a narrower span of control than would be justified, except during some emergency, in organizations where predictable standards can be set and where variances from these standards serve as a basis for corrective actions.

Suojanen's final objection to the span of control principle is that it neglects the role that work groups can play in reducing the work of supervision. He argues that well-knit work groups, accepting company objectives as their own, will settle their own differences and do their own 'policing', thus reducing the need for superiors to be consulted.[21]

Comment on Criticism. It is doubtful whether the arguments on the conflict between a limited span of control and the number of levels is a fundamental one. Although the price of reducing the number of levels is an increase in the span of control, such a reduction may be carried out without increasing the total work load on remaining management. Similarly, although reducing spans of control increases the number of levels, work loads may be decreased without increasing the number of levels. The reason for this is that the work of a supervisor or manager is unlikely to be confined to supervision.

In Fig. 8(*a*), it would be possible to eliminate the whole of management level 'C' to reach the position shown in Fig. 8(*b*),

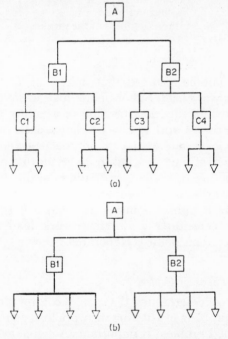

(a)

(b)

FIG. 8.—In (*a*) it would be possible to eliminate the whole of management level 'C' to reach the position shown in (*b*) if 80 per cent of the work of this level could be eliminated or delegated, together with 40 per cent of level 'B'.

if 80 per cent of the work of this level and 40 per cent of the work of level 'B' could be eliminated or delegated to assistants, subordinates or (more likely) to specialists or computer.

That executives do spend their time on activities not associated with supervising immediate subordinates has been demonstrated by research. The table below, showing how fifty-eight executives spent their time, is illustrative.[22]

Chief Executives % of total contacts	Types of contact	Departmental Heads % of total contacts
19	Customers	17½
9	Suppliers	9
1½	Superiors	14½
6	Colleagues	10½
33½	Subordinates	30
6	Mixed status group	6
4	Service department heads	3½
9½	Professional men	4
1½	Other members of the public	5
100	Totals	100

It should not be assumed that delegating to subordinates adds to their work load. Subordinates may waste time waiting for decisions from superiors because of a failure to lay down policy. As Carlson's work in Sweden shows, executives are often caught in a vicious circle; they do not make decisions on policy because of lack of time, but failure to lay down policy leads to further loss of time by both superior and subordinates.[23]

Suojanen's criticism of the span of control principle is more pertinent. He is rightly pointing out that a fixed number of subordinates constitutes a different work load in different circumstances. This point is elaborated below.

Work Load v. Span of Control

The problem of determining the span of control is one factor in the broader problem of assessing the work load on management. This work load problem is important. A company would only need one manager if there was no limit to the load he could bear. Different assessments of the amount of work that can be handled by the average manager create different organization structures.

If the number of relationships supervised is an inadequate determinant of work load, what are the relevant factors? Among the factors are:

1. *The extent to which guidance must be given to subordinates.* The situation may demand step-by-step guidance with the subordinate being continually told what to do and how to do it. On the other hand, only a final check on results may be required. These two situations make different demands on the time of a supervisor or manager. In one analysis, supervisors in the first situation spent five hours per week with each subordinate. In the second situation they spent only one and a half hours per week. For a category falling midway between these two extremes, the time spent was three hours per week.[24] Managerial time can thus be saved by minimising the need for supervision by the following means:

(i) *Training.* Training prepares people to make more decisions for themselves and so reduces the amount of reference to superiors.

(ii) *Co-operation.* Subordinates tend to settle their own work differences or refer them to their superior. Where a co-operative atmosphere exists, management will spend less time settling disputes.

(iii) *Information.* A supervisor or manager may spend time closely directing subordinates. Alternatively, it may be possible to devise an information system that makes clear to the employee the standard demanded and allows the superior merely to concentrate on those cases deviating from standard.

(iv) *Simplifying decision making.* This point is allied to (iii), since information can make decisions more routine by reducing uncertainty. In certain situations, decision making can be considerably simplified by laying down rules detailing the decision to be made for every conceivable situation. In these circumstances there would be little need to consult superiors.

2. *The extent to which the manager is occupied with work other than supervision.* The higher the managerial position, the less is the time spent in supervising immediate subordinates and the more the time devoted to planning.

Work Load as a Basis for Grouping

Work load can be a basis for creating additional levels, sections and departments. Fig. 9(a) represents an organization consisting of four employees and the proprietor. As the organization grows by adding to the number at shop floor level, there may be delegation to a supervisor (Fig. 9*b*). As the organization grows still further, the supervisor becomes overloaded and the work

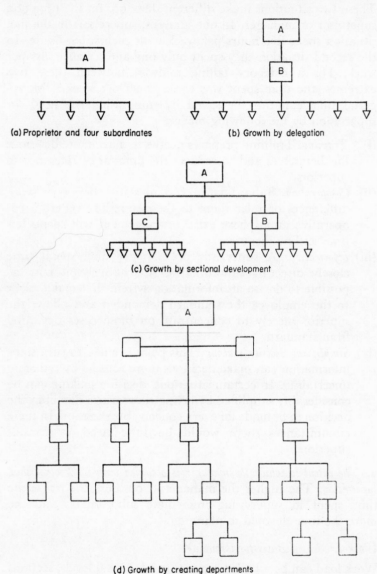

(a) Proprietor and four subordinates

(b) Growth by delegation

(c) Growth by sectional development

(d) Growth by creating departments

FIG. 9.—Grouping as a response to work load.

may be split into sections with separate supervision (Fig. 9c) or grouped into departments (Fig. 9d). Work load by this stage has probably ceased to be a basis for grouping activities directly under some particular executive. Advertising clerks would not be grouped under a production foreman simply to even out supervisory work between production and advertising. Unrelated activities are not grouped under an executive just to provide him with a full work opportunity. On the other hand, work load at any stage can be a reason for not grouping some activity directly under some particular executive. For example, the recent report on Higher Education (the Robbins Report) rejected the suggestion that the Grants Commission for Higher Education should come under the Chancellor of the Exchequer on the ground that it would overburden the Chancellor 'burdened as he is with a host of other responsibilities, it is hard to believe that he can devote to the largest sector of higher education the time or initiative in ministerial discussions that its national importance now demands.'[25]

GROUPING TO ACHIEVE ECONOMIES OF SCALE

When like work is grouped together, then operations are carried out on a larger scale, which may give rise to economies. Grouping to achieve these economies is sometimes known in management literature as grouping by process. A less misleading title is grouping to achieve economies of scale, as this is the term used by economists who must receive credit for giving the most clear statement of these economies. They were first discussed at length by economist J. M. Clark in his *Studies in the Economics of Overhead Cost* published in 1923, and later by Cambridge economist E. A. G. Robinson in his book *The Structure of Competitive Industry* published in 1931.[26, 27]

Robinson lists under five headings the economies arising from the scale of operations; technical, managerial, financial, marketing and risk spreading.

Technical Economies

The technical economies that may arise from increasing the scale of operations are twofold.

(i) *Use of machines.* An expensive machine requires a certain level of output to justify its installation. A section may be formed round the machine, e.g. a computer, and work may be fed to it that was previously carried out by several departments. Even where a large machine can be reproduced on a smaller scale, it may still be more economic to use a larger machine since it may cost less in proportion to run, buy or hire.

(ii) *Increased specialization.* As the scale of operations increases, more opportunity occurs for increased specialization. However, Robinson points out that an increase in the scale of operations can sometimes reverse the tendency to increased specialization, e.g. a punched-card installation may carry out in four or five steps what may have been twelve or more distinct manual operations.

Managerial Economies

If like work is grouped together, there is the possibility of managerial specialization. For example, grouping all accounting together allows one accountant to specialize on income tax, another on management accounting and so on. Such grouping makes better use of scarce specialist knowledge. A company may not be able to afford ten first-class accountants to run ten separate accounting sections spread throughout the company, but may be able to afford one first-class accountant to direct the whole of the company's accounting. As the company grows in size, specialist sections or departments may not need to be increased in the same ratio. For example, if all sales forecasting is grouped together and the firm expands its products, the cost of sales forecasting per unit of product is likely to fall. Such an economy may not arise if each product department has its own forecasting staff.

Financial and Marketing Economies

All buying may be centralized not only to make use of specialist 'know-how' but to obtain trade discounts for bulk purchase. Similarly, the borrowing of funds may be centralized not only to reduce the need for borrowing but also because one department operating for a whole company may be able to influence the interest rate charged and the size of the amount borrowed.

Risk Spreading Economies

Grouping together like activities may lessen the risk of under-employment. The work undertaken by small sections (five or less people) may not quite fully employ a round number of staff. Grouping together several such sections, for example typing pools, may reduce this loss. Grouping together sections whose work flows are complementary may also reduce under-employment. Finally, separate sections performing similar work may be occupied on different products, e.g. one developing colour films and another developing non-colour films. Grouping these sections together means more efficient staffing if demand fluctuates between products.

GROUPING TO ACHIEVE CO-ORDINATION

The greater the degree of co-ordination in an organization, the more individual efforts are integrated during performance rather than reconciled afterwards. The organization structure can facilitate co-ordination as Mary Parker Follett, American political scientist turned management writer, said in 1926:

'You cannot always bring together the results of departmental activities and expect to co-ordinate them. You must have an organization which will permit inter-weaving all along the line. Strand should measure with strand and then we shall not have the clumsy task of trying to patch together finished webs.'[28]

Co-ordination problems increase as a company grows in size. People sharing common goals need to act with knowledge of what colleagues are doing. This is made more difficult as responsibility for meeting goals becomes further subdivided and communication lines multiply and lengthen.

All activities in a company need to be co-ordinated. Hence the need for a chief executive in the role of overall co-ordinator. However, the amount of co-ordination needed between one activity and another will differ. Some activities may be so interdependent that they need a common head to ensure that those concerned with the activities work in unison. A grouping that minimizes co-ordination problems achieves the highest possible degree of self-containment in each of the organization's groupings of activities.

There are a number of signs that point to weak co-ordination.

1. *Lack of consistency in goals.* Lack of co-ordination may mean people are working at cross-purposes to each other. Priorities may differ and conflicting action be taken. For example, a

transport manager may lay down that the cost per mile of making deliveries to any area should never exceed a particular sum, deliveries being delayed until full loads can be sent. This policy may make the transport department appear effective, but the loss from diminished sales through poor customer service may be far higher than the savings made on transport costs.

2. *Non-synchronized timing.* The actions of individuals may not be synchronized or properly scheduled, so that hold-ups and delays occur. For example, a computer installed before the necessary programmes are ready is useless.

3. *Poor specification of duties.* Necessary activities may not be carried out because each person in the team believes it is the responsibility of others. The quality control engineer may lay down standards and assume that the works manager will inform production of the revised standards. Similarly, the works manager may assume that quality control has done the notification.

4. *Lack of economy in means for co-ordination.* Co-ordination is implemented through personal supervision, meetings, liaison personnel, memoranda, procedures and letters. All these means are facilitated or made more difficult and expensive by the organization structure, as this determines the number to be consulted and their accessibility. Hence, even where co-ordination appears satisfactory, it may still be possible to re-group activities to reduce the cost of such co-ordination.

Classical Views

The expression 'grouping to improve co-ordination' is used as a generic expression to cover a number of specific reasons for grouping suggested by classical writers, such as grouping by purpose, to facilitate control, to avoid divided responsibility, and so on.

Fayol argued that activities need to be grouped under one head if they serve some common goal. This was expressed as the Unity of Direction Principle.

'This principle is expressed as: one head and one plan for a group of activities having the same objective. It is the condition essential to unity of action, co-ordination of strength and focusing of effort. A body with two heads is in the social as in the animal sphere a monster, and has difficulty in surviving. Unity of direction (one head one plan) must not be confused with unity of command (one employee to have orders from one superior only). Unity of direction is provided for by sound organization of the body corporate, unity of command turns on the functioning of the personnel. Unity of command cannot exist without unity of direction, but does not flow from it.'[29]

This principle has been misinterpreted by some human relations writers to mean grouping to achieve economies arising from specialization. Thus Argyris of Yale University states:

'If the tasks of everyone in a unit are specialized, then it follows that the objective or purpose of the unit must be specialized. The principle of unity of direction states that administrative and organizational efficiency increases if each unit has a single (or homogeneous set of) activity (activities) that is (are) planned and directed by the leader.'[30]

Criticism of Unity of Direction Principle

The principle is advice at a crude level of generality. Most of the so-called principles suffer similarly. Simon regards them as proverbs and as essentially useless because 'for almost every principle one can find an equally plausible and acceptable contradictory principle'.[31]

Morris of Ohio State University criticizes the principles because they are not stated in the form of hypotheses that can be tested for validity. Thus he comments on the span of control principle or 'law'. 'Aside from the difficulties of obtaining operational definitions for the terms, the law does not predict what will happen if it is not "obeyed" and thus we can hardly tell in application whether it is true or false.'[32]

Bertrand Russell once said of political philosophy: 'The collection of prejudices which is called political philosophy is useful provided that it is not called philosophy'. Similarly, the collection of 'proverbs' called principles of organization can sometimes be useful as a point of departure providing we do not regard them as principles.

All activities within a company can be shown to have common goals provided the goals are stated in sufficiently broad terms. In this sense, the principle merely stresses the need for a single chief executive. The reasoning could be expressed syllogistically as

All activities having the same overall objective must come under one head and share a common plan.
All activities within a company have the same overall objective.
Therefore all activities within a company must come under one head and share a common plan.

Alternatively, the principle is an assumption that:

(i) an overall company objective can be split into distinct goals;
(ii) those activities serving one particular goal can be grouped together to form a unit of the organization.

In other words, although all activities need to be co-ordinated, those activities serving a distinct goal should be co-ordinated first. Grouping and sub-grouping can proceed on this basis. Field selling, field administration, advertising, market research serve a common goal. All help in achieving a certain level of sales or percentage share of the market. Close continuing contact must be maintained to ensure the right 'marketing mix'. Hence the activities may be grouped together to form a marketing department. Since the overall marketing objective can be split into sub-goals, a sub-grouping into sections can be carried out. For example, field sales administration needs to be

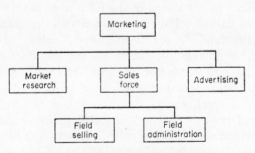

FIG. 10.—A marketing department.

co-ordinated with field selling more than with advertising, hence the grouping could be as in Fig. 10.

The difficulty arises if an activity serves several distinct goals. Under which goal should the activity be grouped? The sharing of a common goal does not help with this problem because it merely indicates the need for co-ordination but does not measure nor show the nature of that need.

Where the pattern of interdependence between activities is relatively stable and predictable, then it may be possible to carry out co-ordination by planning well in advance. People thus know what to expect of each other without being grouped under a common head. On the other hand, where the pattern of interdependence is relatively unstable, then close continuing contact may be necessary. Such a situation may require that the activities be grouped together under a common head.

GROUPING BY NATURE OF ACTIVITY

The 'keyness' of an activity and the function it performs influence the level at which grouping takes place.

Keyness of Activity

'Key' activities demand 'key' attention, and higher management may wish to directly supervise these activities. Hence they may be grouped under them.

(i) Activities that bind the company long term, such as finance concerned with large capital projects, may come under the chief executive.

(ii) Those that are of a delicate qualitative nature, for example certain aspects of labour relations, may come under the chief executive.

(iii) Those where failure could have wide repercussions or result in considerable loss, such as advertising, may not be grouped with other marketing activities but may have a separate head responsible directly to the chief executive. It would be up to the chief executive to co-ordinate advertising with the rest of marketing before co-ordinating both these activities with other functions of the company.

Where a 'key' activity is separated in the management hierarchy from those activities with which it most needs to be co-ordinated, there is a danger that co-ordination will be weak. An example from education is given in the Robbins Report, which recommended that there should be one Minister of Arts and Sciences responsible for the autonomous educational institutions and certain other matters and another minister responsible for the rest of education. Such a recommendation was made in the belief that both parts of education warranted a separate chief with independent access to the Cabinet. The creation of two Ministers of Education would have increased the problem of co-ordinating the whole field of education. Expansion in the field of higher education depends on supporting development in the schools so that there is a need for co-ordinated development programmes. How could this co-ordination be achieved with two separate ministers if the idea of the Cabinet itself fulfilling the role is rejected? If this problem occurred in a company three courses would be possible.

1. Co-ordination could be left to the departments themselves to work out.
2. One of the departmental heads could be assigned the task of achieving co-ordination.
3. The chief common to both ministers or departmental heads could carry out the co-ordination. Alternatively, a common chief could be appointed.

Each of these solutions will be considered in turn.

Co-ordination left to Departments. Where co-ordination is left to the units themselves, each head is expected to consult other departmental heads about common problems. Usually some administrative machinery, such as a committee, is set up to look into proposals on behalf of all units and to ensure that all heads are involved in suggested changes. Basically this was the solution of the Robbins Report. Co-ordination was to be left to the two ministers helped by advisory and consultative committees who would survey the field of education as a whole.

The Report argued that co-ordination would still be necessary even with one minister. There is a failure in this argument to perceive the advantages of having one man in charge. There are distinct advantages in grouping highly interdependent activities under one head. With two ministers, no one person would be responsible for formulating an overall education objective and no one person responsible for the completeness of a co-ordinated education programme. It would be no one minister's responsibility to look at education as a whole so opportunities may be missed and only pressing problems solved. Furthermore, no one minister could be held responsible for progress on matters of joint concern and one ministry could delay progress by holding back its contribution. On difficult 'political' issues there might be no progress, each waiting for the other to take the initiative. Finally, if industrial experience is any guide (for example when advertising and the rest of marketing have separate chiefs responsible only to the board), having separate ministries could lead to the duplication of effort. Staff in both ministries might carry out similar work on problems before consulting the joint advisory bodies.

Co-ordination assigned to one of the Departmental Heads. An example from business would be the situation in which the head of accounts was given responsibility for all interdepartmental clerical procedures, e.g. order handling system. There is a danger in this arrangement that other departmental heads might regard suggestions from the accountant as merely reflections of vested interest and prejudice. A similar position might arise if one of two ministers of equal status was given the responsibility of achieving co-ordination.

Common Chief to carry out the Co-ordination. Highly interdependent activities may require a common chief though he may be helped by staff acting on his behalf. The appointment of a common head, however, does not guarantee co-ordination. He may abrogate his responsibility and misguidedly follow in practice solutions similar to those discussed.

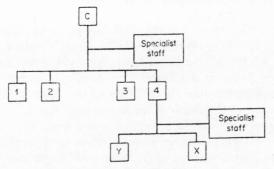

FIG. 11.—Co-ordination.

Function of Activity

It was stated earlier that a co-ordinating head may have staff helping him to co-ordinate. This staff should be grouped with him.

For example, in Fig. 11 the co-ordinator of departments 1, 2, 3, and 4 is 'C'. Clerical procedures that are common to these departments help 'C' in his job of co-ordination. Where such procedures are defective, co-ordination is impaired. As a consequence, any specialist staff undertaking analysis of inter-departmental procedures should be attached to 'C' as this staff acts on his behalf. Similarly, any specialist staff undertaking analysis of procedures confined to units X and Y should be attached to the manager of department 4.

CONFLICT OF FACTORS

The four factors relevant to grouping—span of control, economies of scale, co-ordination, nature of activity—can pull in opposite directions from each other. A solution, for example, that reduces overall cost by reaping economies of scale may nevertheless increase co-ordination costs.

Sometimes conflicts cause little difficulty. Few companies would group market research under accounting because economies of scale are possible through better utilization of calculating machines. Sometimes conflicts can be resolved if co-ordination can be planned. The training of salesmen can be taken as an example. Such training, if carried out by Sales, ensures close co-ordination with field selling. On the other hand, better training facilities might be available in Personnel where large-scale training is undertaken. In this case no conflict need exist.

Sales could draw up the syllabus in conjunction with Personnel but delegate the training to them. No changes in the syllabus would be made without approval from Sales. Co-ordination between Sales and Personnel can be achieved by such planning because the stability of the sales training pro-gramme lessens the need for frequent consultation.

A major difficulty in grouping arises when one grouping improves co-ordination in one direction and weakens it in another. Companies tend to organize their major groupings on what is termed a functional basis, such as marketing, produc-tion, accounting and so on, though there is much argument over the grouping of minor functions, such as warehousing. Such functional grouping may achieve economies of scale and co-ordination of a function company-wide, but it does make acute the problem of co-ordination between functions. As Robinson states 'each department will be invaded by numerous outside experts, decisions affecting his department will be made by others than the head of the department concerned, and the co-ordination of the various authorities within each individual department will be more difficult and demand more diplomacy . . .'.[33]

CO-ORDINATION AND COMMITTEES

Committees are widely used in business to help co-ordinate activities. They tend either to be strongly advocated or strongly condemned for reasons such as the following:

For	Against
(a) Committee decision represents the combined judgment of members.	(a) Committee decision represents compromise or simply the dominance of the Chairman.
(b) Committees improve communication and liaison within and between departments.	(b) Committees undermine the individual manager.
(c) Committees develop teamwork and broaden individual managers, making them appreciate the operating problems of their colleagues.	(c) Committees are wasteful in time—'make minutes and waste hours'.

In general, committees are useful for gaining acceptance of ideas since they provide an opportunity for reconciling viewpoints and for bringing social pressure to bear on those who unreasonably oppose change or those who unreasonably propose it. They are also valuable in helping management formulate plans. On the other hand, it is more satisfactory to hold a single individual accountable for performance since committees have 'neither souls to be damned nor bodies to be kicked'.

The success of a committee often depends on its composition and the manner in which it is run. A committee should have a definite brief and, ideally, be limited to about five people. The following table suggests the uses of committees.

Advising Management.	Excellent
Gaining acceptance	Fair
Communication vehicle	Fair
Fact collection	Poor
Implementing decisions	Poor

D

CO-ORDINATION AND DIVISIONALIZATION

The problem of co-ordination between functions becomes more difficult as a company grows in size. As the number of workers and management levels increases, units become more remote from top management co-ordination and less in sympathy with the needs of other departments. In certain circumstances this position may be relieved by divisionalization. Where a company makes several products which can be separated on a basis of technology or market, the company may be split into divisions for each distinct product or market.

Where a company makes several distinct products there may be few economies of scale resulting from grouping all manufacturing activities together or all sales activities together. There may be a far greater need to co-ordinate activities associated with each product than there is to co-ordinate activities common to all products. In these circumstances, product divisionalization might improve co-ordination (Fig. 12a). It involves separating all major activities associated with a product group into one unit, for instance ICI has a Pharmaceuticals Division, a Paints Division and so on.

Divisionalization may also be on a geographic basis (Fig. 12b). This involves dividing the market into regions, each containing all the major activities necessary for producing and selling. Geographic divisionalization may be the only way of extending sales over a wider market area. For instance, a bread manufacturer who wishes to have nationwide sales may divisionalize geographically because of the cost of transporting bread and the risk of deterioration during travel.

Divisionalization may be mixed. Manufacturing may be broken up into separate units on the basis of product but sales may be split on a geographical basis. With divisionalization there remains the problem of achieving co-ordination between divisions and co-ordinating specialist functions company-wide.

DELEGATING AUTHORITY

As a company grows from a one-man business the proprietor is obliged to delegate part of his work to others. In the process he delegates some of his authority. Authority can be defined as the institutionalized right to make decisions and give orders on behalf of the organization. Under this definition the source of authority is the institutions of society, particularly the institution of private property.

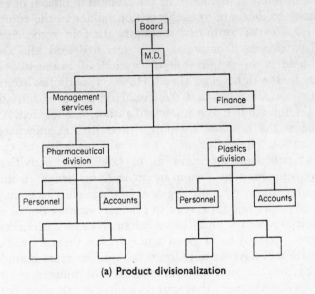

(a) **Product divisionalization**

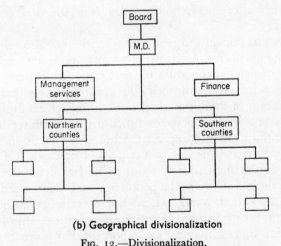

(b) **Geographical divisionalization**

FIG. 12.—Divisionalization.

Fayol himself defined authority as 'the right to give orders and the power to exact obedience'. He also made a distinction between a manager's *official* authority 'derived from office' and *personal* authority 'compounded of intelligence, experience, moral worth, ability to lead, past services, etc.'.[34]

One problem is to determine the amount of official or formal authority to delegate to each position holder in the company. The exercise of authority manifests itself in some form of activity. Hence, if activities were specified and allocated to office-holders in detail, the delegation of authority would merely be the right to go ahead. However, activities are not so specified or allocated and the broad grouping of activities is only a rough guide to the amount of authority delegated. A man can be at the head of a group of activities as shown on an organization chart but may have no authority to change current practices. Decisions as to how these activities are carried out may be taken by executives remote from the particular unit, e.g. all regional selling activities may be grouped under one supervisor but he may or may not be given authority to engage and dismiss salesmen or to authorize their expenses. Even if he is given authority on these matters, the authority will have definite limits though the exact boundaries may be only vaguely known to him. The more a person is supervised—whether that supervision is exercised before, during or after performance—the less the delegation of authority.

The factors relevant to grouping activities are also relevant to delegating authority. A central buyer may be given sole buying authority, to reap economies of scale. Another expert at head office may be given authority to ensure the company-wide co-ordination of some function, accounting for example, or to achieve co-ordination between functions, for instance between production and marketing. Furthermore, if a decision is 'key', authority to make the decision is pushed upwards. Of course, the cost of decision making tends to be less if the decision is made at the point where the problem arises rather than higher up. On the other hand, where the exercise of authority is infrequent, for example in determining recruitment policy, the actual decision cost may not be important. Far more important may be the difference in effectiveness and speed between one person and another being authorized to make a decision.

Classical writers give varied advice on the problem of delegating authority. Some argue that authority 'to take or initiate action should be delegated as close to the scene of action as possible'.[35] A recent view is that stated by Allen and also by Koontz and O'Donnell:

'Perhaps the most important guiding principle of delegation is that authority should be delegated to the extent and in the way necessary for the accomplishment of results expected. Too many managers try to partition and define authorities for their subordinates on the basis of how much power can be delegated, or how much withheld, rather than looking first at the job they expect their subordinates to do and then determining how much authority is necessary for them to accomplish the task.'[36]

Unfortunately, it may be unwise to state what is expected from a subordinate without first considering the consequences of giving him the requisite authority. Any original allocation of goals may be modified after such consideration.

There is a danger that a manager is held accountable for results when his control over the factors that influence these results is minimal. Because of this Taylor, Fayol, Urwick and others have argued for the principle that authority should be commensurate with responsibility. For example, it would seem wrong to hold a production manager accountable for material costs when he has no authority over the purchasing of materials other than to provide specifications. However, Mason Haire of the University of California comments on this principle as follows:

'One of the most persistent repetitions in the mythology of organization theory is the notion that the authority attached to a position must be commensurate with responsibility. It appears in almost every textbook and has done so for so long that it is accepted without question. It seems to be a truism among organizational principles. This happens even though there seems to be no other human relationship in which the amount of authority one has is closely related to his responsibility. Certainly the citizen's responsibility far exceeds his authority in breadth and amount. Similarly, the church-member's, the neighbor's, and, perhaps most of all, the parent's authority seems to be least just when his responsibility is greatest. Why, in this one situation, should it be so carefully equalized? The argument seems to be that it is not right for a man to be responsible for something over which he has no authority. But this seems to impose a special meaning on both authority and responsibility.

'If by "responsibility" one means that the incumbent is completely answerable for the success or failure of an operation, then he must, to protect himself, limit his responsibility to those things over which he has a direct and immediate control. This kind of sense of responsibility must surely work against the general goals of the organization. We want him to feel the broadest possible responsibility for the objectives and activities of the firm. The narrower interpretation of responsibility leads to the frequent—and frequently expensive—practice of saying, "I only did what I was supposed to do. If someone else didn't, or if my part didn't fit in, it's no business of mine." This is the exact opposite of a general commitment to the organization. It is part of a long tradition of evading responsibility by circumscribing responsibility—from Pontius Pilate to the generals who excused war crimes by saying they did what they were told.

' "Authority", too, to fit this scheme, must have a special meaning. It is only conferred authority—the authority of the position—that is subject to this kind of manipulation in measured amounts. It leaves out of account the degree to which one may discharge his responsibilities by exercising his influence rather than authority, by personal authority (rather than conferred), and by the shared objectives of his working group. Just as the narrow interpretation of responsibility worked against the organizational objectives by inhibiting a general commitment, the narrow interpretation of authority seems to do so by concentrating on a single kind of authority and not by utilizing the sources of power in the leader himself and his relation with his working group.

'It is not at all clear how one computes the calculus that lies behind commensurate authority and responsibility. If a salesman's territory is doubled (in size? in dollar volume? in potential?) should his authority be doubled, too? What is twice as much authority in such a case? We often can reduce it to a commitment authority—the right to spend so and so much without higher approval—and thus get at least a neat scale that can be doubled and halved at will. But, on the one hand, this commitment authority is very little of the manager's authority, and, on the other, it is the most common of dodges to go beyond the intended authority by repeated commitments.

The calculus implied by the principle seems virtually impossible in practice.

'The idea seems to have persisted because it fits in with an accounting approach to organization. In a neat bookkeeping-like structure, a balance is maintained by putting in a certain amount of authority and expecting out a certain amount of responsibility. This gives a neat, clear, comprehensible, and controllable system. It also limits responsibility and inhibits general commitment and initiative while it narrows the meaning of authority within the structure. If only in the interest of strengthening these latter points, it seems worth while to challenge the persistent myth.'[37]

In the above passage Haire confuses responsibility to oneself with responsibility to superiors. A junior manager may feel responsible to himself for the whole future of his company but would be highly indignant if higher management held him responsible for that future. In any case, it is difficult to understand the suggested corollary to Haire's arguments that providing people are not held accountable they will have a broad commitment to the general goals of the company and not limit their responsibility simply to those things over which they have direct and immediate control. Also, it is difficult to understand how delegating formal authority inhibits general commitment to organizational objectives simply because it does not tell the executive how to use his personal qualities and relations with work groups. Finally, Haire makes the point about measurement as if responsibility and authority needed to be measured on a ratio scale before the principle could have any real application in practice. It is not necessary to measure authority to ascertain whether enough authority has been given for the carrying out of some particular task.

DECENTRALIZATION AND DIVISIONALIZATION

The problem of delegating authority is associated with the problem of decentralization. Decentralization can be defined as the systematic delegation of authority to all organization units and centralization as the tendency to withhold such authority. Unfortunately, the terms remain vague concepts. A company whose top management regards it as decentralized may be viewed as highly centralized by an outsider or by lower levels within the company. Allen distinguishes decentralization from divisionalization. He argues that although divisionalization facilitates decentralization, there can be decentralization without divisionalization.

A division cannot be granted complete autonomy. As Allen states: 'a division cannot be permitted to bankrupt a company or to grow to the detriment of the group as a whole.'[38]

As a minimum, central headquarters need to:

(i)   approve the objectives of each division since these need to be compatible with overall aims;

(ii) approve divisional organization structure including 'key' appointments.

The gains from retaining authority at central headquarters need to be set against the losses arising from poorer co-ordination at the local level.

Gains

(i) *Economies of scale*: a motor-car company may have a number of divisions where each division manufactures a different type of vehicle; if most of the vehicles are made from parts which are interchangeable between models, central authority may insist on controlling car design.

(ii) *Co-ordination*: advertising may be centralized so as to reap the benefits of co-ordinated, large scale, national advertising.

(iii) *Nature of activity*: all negotiations with unions over working conditions or wages may be done by management at central headquarters.

Losses

There is always a danger in retaining authority centrally that local management is reduced to doing little more than maintaining an existing machinery, all changes being authorized by others. This can be frustrating to divisional management. Furthermore, the higher the degree of centralization, the more is the possibility of delay in decision making. However, such a possibility can be anticipated and plans for centralization modified, e.g. although some functions such as purchasing may be done centrally in order to reap economies of scale, it is common to allow deviations for specific reasons. Thus one

Swiss firm set up a central purchasing department (CPD), but made the following stipulation:

'In setting up the CPD, our management intended to create a centralized office that would deal with all purchasing and services as economically as possible. There was no intention, however, to bureaucratize the purchasing function and make it inflexible and clumsy.

'In order to ensure continued flexibility, certain powers were delegated to the factories; they may—but need not—make use of these facilities. They are authorized to place

(*a*) small orders, value below SFr 100,
(*b*) urgent orders in emergencies (e.g. risk of a production stoppage),
(*c*) orders for furniture and fittings for company-owned flats,
(*d*) subscriptions and orders for books,
(*e*) orders for gardening requisites,
(*f*) orders for private staff purchases.

'They are also authorized to buy direct from handicapped suppliers (e.g. the blind).

'The delegation of these powers has contributed to a smooth relationship between the works and the CPD.'[39]

SPECIFYING RESPONSIBILITY

Side by side with authority is the concept of responsibility. As Fayol said:

'Authority is not to be conceived of apart from responsibility, that is apart from sanction—reward or penalty—which goes with the exercise of power. Responsibility is a corollary of authority, it is its natural consequence and essential counterpart, and wheresoever authority is exercised responsibility arises.'[40]

There is no general agreement on a definition of responsibility. It can be defined, as used in this book, as the obligation to carry out certain activities with accountability for performance. Thus Koontz and O'Donnell define responsibility as 'the obligation of a subordinate to whom a superior has assigned a duty to perform the service required'.[41] However, Allen and others have defined responsibility merely as the mental and physical acts a person is expected to carry out. This controversy over definition gives rise to debate as to whether responsibility can be delegated. If responsibility is defined in the first sense, then it cannot be delegated since delegation down the line merely creates additional responsibility but does not absolve the delegator from his responsibilities. On the other hand, if responsibility is defined merely in the sense of duties, then it manifestly can be delegated. The first definition is used in these pages so that responsibility is spoken of as being created rather than delegated.

Great emphasis is placed in the classical approach on clearly defining each manager's responsibilities. Written definitions are usually advocated. Brech, for example, states

'It is the contention of the present author that the responsibilities of management forming an organization structure should always be written down in properly constituted statements or "schedules". This, it is maintained, is the only practical means of delegation, the only effective way of making known the pattern of responsibilities and relationships, both to the holders of the positions concerned and to all others who together form the management team.'[42]

Bennett in a publication for the American Management Association reproduces about 150 illustrative schedules. He distinguishes the 'managerial position description' from the job description used at shop floor level . . .

'there is less stress on the mechanics of how a man goes about doing his work (his day-to-day duties and assignments) and more emphasis on the position's responsibilities, the contribution the work makes to the firm's welfare, and the impact on the company's operations. The descriptions are usually written in more general terms, and they tend to give greater weight to relationships and lines of authority (how a position fits in to the overall corporate scheme) rather than to internal, self-contained duties of a particular position.'[43]

There are a number of reasons for advocating these schedules or position descriptions.

(i) Vague assignments of responsibility make for confusion, recrimination and jurisdictional conflict. These dangers are said to outweigh the possibility that position descriptions leave the way open for not doing something because it was not specifically defined.

(ii) Unless a person knows his responsibilities it is unfair to hold him accountable for non-performance.

(iii) They can be used not only to communicate duties, authority and responsibilities, but also in making comparisons between jobs for salary scale purposes and for anticipating the future need for managers.

(iv) Clear assignments can limit interference from superiors. On this particular point, the following quotation from Sherwood and Pfiffner is appropriate:

'There is an impression in some of the literature on bureaucracy, as well as in popular writings, that formalization may be a stultifying influence. Bakke's study of the Southern New England Telephone Company, however, reports one unexpected finding. In that organization detailed job descriptions were used for assignment purposes and as vehicles for drill during training sessions. The researchers expected that the workers would find such descriptions restrictive of freedom, but actually the effect was the opposite, for two reasons. First, knowing what is expected of him, the employee is subjected to less close supervision. Immediate supervisors have fewer excuses to interfere with what he is doing. Second, his knowledge of what is expected of him gives the employee sufficient feeling of security to devise and invent informal working patterns which are in harmony with the written word. Thus, job descriptions facilitate delegation and operate to discourage that type of oversupervision manifested by a superior's undue interference in a subordinate's work. The latter has written authority for resisting such oversupervision.'[44]

The AMA manual breaks down a position description into the following categories.

1. *Function* (also called 'purpose of the Job', 'Basic Function', and 'Objective'). This section serves as a summary of, and general introduction to, the position under consideration by stating its basic purposes briefly and in very direct language.

2. *Duties and/or Responsibilities* (also called 'Major', 'Specific' or 'Basic Duties and/or Responsibilities' and sometimes

'Principal Activities'). This section enumerates the principal specific duties and responsibilities which must be met by the incumbent in order to fulfil his basic function as outlined in the description.

3. *Authority* (also called 'Limits of Authority'). This section sets the limits to which an executive may go in order to perform his duties. It specifies the exact extent of an incumbent's power or authority in so far as this is possible. Some participants regard this section as the 'charter' or 'grant of authority' under which a manager operates. Since many companies feel that responsibilities and authority are inextricably interdependent, the sections labelled 'Duties and Responsibilities' and 'Authority' are, in many descriptions, combined into one large section.

4. *Relationships* (also called 'Organizational', 'Reporting' or 'Working Relationships' and sometimes 'Supervision exercised'). This section describes relationships that are vital to the accomplishment of the manager's work. Sometimes the description is limited to outlining relationships within the company—on the incumbent's own level, with those above him and those below him.

5. *Other sections.* In addition to the above major elements, some descriptions also contain sections designed to aid in measuring the incumbent's performance; these are most commonly called 'Standards of Performance'.[45]

Brech follows similar lines in recommending the following:

1. *A Heading* to include: Title of Appointment
To whom responsible
A code reference
Date of issue

2. *Main List of Responsibilities* under the caption 'Responsible for . . .'.

3. A Section called *Special Responsibilities* that sets out items a little aside from the main field to which particular attention is called.

4. *Limitations*: a full note of any things immediately relevant to the executive's field of activities, but for which he is to have no

authority, or which he is asked not to do, because they are covered elsewhere.

5. *Subordinates*: a list of the responsible members of staff directly responsible to him.

6. *Functional Contacts*: the other executives or the specialists with whom he is to make contacts in relation to the co-ordination of their respective fields in relation to services requested.

7. *Committees*: a note of any committee on which the executive is to serve as a member as of right, or co-opted, or called in for attendance (see Fig. 13).

EXAMPLE OF SCHEDULE OF RESPONSIBILITIES

Title: Sales Director.

Responsible to: Managing Director.

Responsible for:
1. The overall direction and co-ordination of the Sales and Advertising Departments.
2. Communication of Board Policy and decisions to Advertising and Sales Management.
3. Interpreting Board Policy to Advertising and Sales Management in cases where that policy is not explicit.
4. Ensuring that the actions of subordinates lie within the agreed policy of the Board.
5. Constantly reviewing the procedures of the Sales and Advertising Departments to ensure that operations are carried out at a minimum cost.
6. Submitting for Board approval such changes in Sales, Advertising or Distribution policy as suggested by research and changing market conditions.
7. Presenting to the Board reports showing the current trading position and the effectiveness of Sales and Advertising policies.

Special Duties:
1. Submission of Sales and Advertising Expenditure Budgets.
2. Negotiations and liaison with Advertising Agents to ensure advertising expenditure used to give maximum effect.
3. Board Member responsibilities.

Immediate Subordinates:
H. T. Sales Manager
Advertising Manager
Office Manager
Head of Sales Research.

FIG. 13.—Example of schedule of responsibilities.

It is interesting to note that President Franklin Roosevelt refused to define the apportionment of responsibilities among the agencies of his administration. This gave rise to conflicts which could only be resolved by the President himself. In this way he kept himself informed as to what was going on in his administration.[46]

An objection to many current job descriptions is that they are inadequate. Few stress job objectives and fewer state how performance is to be assessed. Finally, insufficient attention is paid to the subtlety of the decision-making process so that many job descriptions are ambiguous as to precisely what decision-making authority has been delegated.

ESTABLISHING RELATIONSHIPS

When the work of a company is divided into distinct operating units, there is a need to get the divided parts working together. In order to achieve this co-ordination, people within a company may need to be formally related to each other so that each knows his position in the team. Unfortunately, the literature on the subject of these formal relationships abounds in confusion as writers mix up relationships between people with relationships between departments. The relationships between two people will first be discussed.

The Line Relationship. Each person below the chief executive is accountable to someone else. This is the line or command relationship and is the relationship between superior and subordinate. Since each supervisor or manager has a line relationship between himself and his subordinates and between himself and his superior, a chain of command is established from top to bottom in any company. Emphasis is placed on specifying the line relationship because it establishes

(i)   the official lines of communication from top to bottom in an organization,
(ii) to whom each subordinate is accountable,
(iii) those responsible for co-ordinating each subordinate's efforts with work carried out by others.

The Unity of Command principle is often quoted in connection with the line relationship: No member of an organization should be held accountable to more than one superior though he may have to conform to the standing or periodic instructions of people other than his superior.

This definition puts the most favourable interpretation on the principle. An alternative interpretation—that an employee should receive orders from only one person—has been subject to criticism in that adherence to the principle would rule out giving instructions to other than one's own subordinates.

For example, X in Fig. 14 could represent the accounting function. When the organization was first set up, X might have

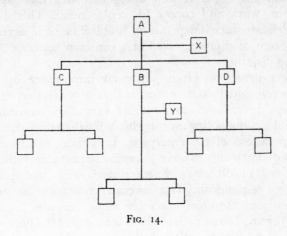

FIG. 14.

framed instructions for A to approve and send out to B. As accounting procedures became established, A might have authorized X to issue orders direct to B to save time. None the less, if B receives an instruction from X which he believes is inconsistent with A's intentions or wrong in some other way, he can protest to X. If there is disagreement, B can appeal to A, who alone can discipline B and settle conflicts between his two subordinates. A great deal of confusion arises through failure to recognize that a subordinate need not be held account-able for carrying out an instruction to the same person who issued the instruction.

The Unity of Command principle and the principle that authority should be commensurate with responsibility are not, of course, unrelated. The chairman of a Watch Committee opposed the suggestion that the Home Secretary should have increased powers over local police forces on the ground that

Watch Committees cannot assume responsibility for the efficiency
of a force if they cannot make the chief constable accountable
to the Committee. This Chairman felt, like Fayol, that dual
command results in an undermining of authority and a
disruption in discipline.

The Unity of Command principle is, however, violated to
achieve better co-ordination. For example, X could represent
the head of work study and Y a work study man attached to
B's department. X may be authorized to lay down how Y
carries out his work. X and B together will then assess Y,
assign him work and choose his replacement. This situation
can be delicate since it depends on X and B being in agreement.
In the event of disagreement their common superior A must
settle the dispute.

Another principle, given particular importance by Brech,
which is relevant to this section is that organization at board
level should create a single chief executive (co-ordinator)
responsible to the policy forming body for the effective conduct
of all operations of the enterprise. It is more satisfactory for
heads of departments to have to report to one man rather than
to a board of directors. Furthermore, with a single chief
executive, responsibility for overall co-ordination remains
undivided and the chief executive alone becomes responsible
for interpreting board policy. His task is to find the best balance
between the various units of the organization so that each
makes a maximum contribution to achieving objectives. He
also has another role. He gives personality to the enterprise.
The image he creates often becomes the image of the company.

Peter Drucker would qualify the principle of a single chief
executive. He argues that the chief executive in the large company needs to be a team though he acknowledges that within
this team there must be a 'Captain who is more than one among
equals', and each member of the team should have 'assigned
to him the areas in which he makes formal decisions and for
which he is responsible'.[47]

Functional Relationship. A manager may not have full authority
to act in all matters concerning the organization unit under him.

1. He may delegate some of his own authority to subordinates
and may not wish to undermine them by withdrawing some
portion of it.

2. He is subject to certain legal restrictions.

3. He is subject to certain informal restrictions in that from experience he knows that certain actions would not be acceptable to subordinates.

4. Higher management may hold back some authority or, in certain cases, delegate some of that authority to others so that people other than the manager and his subordinates have a say in the activities of the unit. To return to Fig. 14, X may have a hand in making decisions relating to the activities grouped under B.

(i) X may be given some authority over Y to facilitate the company-wide co-ordination of the function carried out by X and Y.

(ii) X may be given authority to enter B, C and D's departments to investigate and make recommendations to A on matters that are of common concern to all departments, that is to say matters that are concerned with the co-ordination of departments B, C and D.

(iii) B may not be allowed to carry out certain activities that would logically come under him. X may carry out these activities on his behalf to reap (say) the economies of central buying.

(iv) X may simply provide facts to A and B, for example market research findings. Even in this case X has some influence since his information cannot continue to be ignored if it can be shown that, if followed, it would improve decision making.

In all these four cases X is said to have a functional relationship to B. As can be seen, the functional relationship is not purely advisory but often involves the exercise of authority though the authority is both specialist and restricted.

Personal Assistant. A person may be related to his superior by giving him and him alone general help with his managerial work. Personal assistants are often advocated to relieve the burden on management, or as a training ground. A number of personal assistants allocated to a manager can be a reflection on his ability to delegate. Where each such assistant specializes, e.g. one in sales, one in finance, etc., the authority of the heads of these specialist functions can be undermined. There is also

E

the danger that the personal assistant might abuse his position by exercising authority to which he is not entitled.

Lateral Relationships. All the relationships so far described can be laid down formally and written into management position guides. However, people at roughly the same hierarchical level communicate informally to co-ordinate their individual efforts. The production supervisor in one department will get in touch with his opposite number in another department to settle interdepartmental problems. On minor issues, it would be wasteful in time and resources to settle all problems at the level where the two departments have a common co-ordinator, so informal relationships develop to solve these problems. These lateral relationships, as they are called, are often encouraged to minimise 'red tape'. Thus Urwick comments: 'It is both right and proper that every organization should have its formal scalar chain, just as every well-built house has its drainage system. But it is as unnecessary to use the formal channels exclusively or primarily as the sole means of communication as it is unnecessary to pass one's time in the drains.'[48]

Relationships between departments. It is convenient to distinguish between those departments which create and sell the company's products and those that provide specialist services. Sometimes the terms 'line' and 'staff' are used to distinguish these two groups but to avoid ambiguity the terms 'operational' and 'specialist' are preferable since a line relationship exists within each specialist department and the term staff is often used in the sense of those not paid on an hourly basis.

It is sometimes argued that people in specialist departments have no authority but only advise and persuade. On this issue Haire comments: 'Yet, if authority is commensurate with responsibility, no authority must surely mean no responsibility!'[49]

Haire commits the fallacy of replacing the meaning of a word used in one context with an allied but different meaning. Some writers have indeed claimed, wrongly, that people in specialist departments should have no authority but the context would suggest that they mean 'authority over staff in operational departments' so that unity of command is not undermined. There has never been any suggestion that management in specialist departments should have no authority over their own staff or that a buyer is not exercising authority when he spends thousands of pounds of company money per day.

WORK ORGANIZATION

(Organizing Work at Shop Floor Level)

The problem of work organization lies in grouping tasks to form individual jobs. This problem is ignored by most of the major classical writers when writing on organization. Either it was not considered to be an organization problem or it was believed to be simply an application of the principle of specialization. In recent years the problem has been considered by human relations writers. They rightly point out that traditional management literature has emphasized the advantages of specialization. Thus Urwick quotes from Taylor and comments as follows:

'F. W. Taylor, again, adds a most important subsidiary principle to this one of functional differentiation—the principle of specialization. "The work of every person in the organization should be confined as far as possible to the performance of a single leading function." More waste and friction occurs in human organizations through failure to observe this principle, and there is more to be gained by its careful application than in any other single direction. In one sense, it is only immemorial wisdom—"let the cobbler stick to his last".'[50]

Adam Smith, the eighteenth-century economist, was the first to analyse the contribution to industrial efficiency made by specialization. Since the time of Adam Smith, specialization has become more developed with work being split into progressively finer divisions so that even the old model T Ford was the product of 7,882 different jobs.[51]

Specialization brings a number of benefits.

(i) *Use of scarce ability*. Specialization provides greater opportunity for utilizing scarce ability and provides opportunity for people to follow their natural bent.

(ii) *Development of skill*. Limiting the range of activities undertaken increases the opportunity for developing skill. The specialist typist will generally type more skilfully than the general-purpose clerk.

(iii) *Reduction of training*. Training a man to carry out several tasks generally takes longer than training him to carry out one task. Where labour turnover is high there is an incentive to make specialization as narrow as possible so that training is minimized.

(iv) *Changeover time reduced.* Less time is spent moving from one task to another. In the changeover, a man 'commonly saunters a little. . . When he first begins he is seldom very keen and hearty; his mind, as they say, does not go to it, and for some time he rather trifles than applies to good purpose.' (Adam Smith, *Wealth of Nations.*)

(v) *Higher machine utilization.* In a situation where all do the same work and machinery is used periodically, a decision must be made as to whether (*a*) to provide each employee with the appropriate machinery, (*b*) to allow queueing for the available machines, or (*c*) to schedule machine time. Thus non-specialization in certain circumstances can mean low machine utilization or time wasted in queueing or scheduling.

(vi) *Mechanization.* Finally, specialization encourages mechanization as well as vice versa. As Cairncross the economist states:

'Now if every stage of manufacture from start to finish were in the hands of the same worker, it would be very difficult to disentangle the mechanical operations and turn them over to a machine. For the machinery necessary for a single stage in manufacture is very often much too expensive to be worth introducing unless it is kept in constant use, and it is likely to be capable of handling an output far greater than a single worker could cope with.'[52]

Specialization does not increase efficiency indefinitely. It may be decreasing cost in one direction but adding more in another. Increasing specialization increases interdependence, thus making co-ordination more difficult. As Robinson states:

'Every time that a further division of labour is introduced, every time that a job which was previously done by one man or one group of men is divided into two or more parts, the problem of co-ordinating the work of the now separated groups or individuals begins to arise.'[53]

A similar point is made by Urwick:

'In the second place the time and effort expended in securing that a partially processed piece of work passes from desk to desk

or bench to bench, and often from room to room, where a
highly subdivided chain of processes is applied to large-scale
production of any kind, may well exceed the economy on each
individual process secured by subdivision. Where each new
worker, as with many clerical tasks, has to secure some grasp
of the details of the job as a whole, the time this takes has to be
multiplied by the number of processes the individual item passes
through. Observation of Government Departments handling
large numbers of individual cases suggests that there is insufficient appreciation of these limitations of the principle of subdivision of labour.

'In other words, planning is not an end in itself. Frequently
there is far too little planning. But such planning as is necessary
and desirable is nevertheless an on-cost, and for that reason to
be avoided where possible.'[54]

As co-ordination becomes more difficult, more supervision
may be required. Even so there may still be bottlenecks due to
imperfections in the balancing of work among different team
members.

An example may help to illustrate the problem of determining the degree of specialization. Fig. 15 represents a section

Operation No.	Minutes per Operation	Number of Operators	$\dfrac{B}{C}$	Total Unoccupied Time $(4{\cdot}8-D)\times(C)$
(A)	(B)	(C)	(D)	(E)
1	13·5	3	4·5	·9
2	3·1	1	3·1	1·7
3	6·6	2	3·3	3·0
4	3·9	1	3·9	·9
5	4·8	1	4·8	—
6	3·6	1	3·6	1·2
Totals	35·5	9	—	7·7

$$\therefore \text{Production per eight-hour day} = \frac{60}{(35{\cdot}5+7{\cdot}7)}\times 8\times 9$$
$$= 100 \text{ units}$$

FIG. 15.

employing nine people engaged in carrying out a job broken
down into six tasks. The table shows that the total job takes

35·5 minutes of work but 43·2 minutes to complete because 7·7 minutes is unoccupied because of poor team balancing.

If one person could be trained to carry out the operations at the times listed in Column B, the output per eight-hour day, for the nine-man section (assuming that no additional time was spent in changing over from one operation to the next), would be

$$\frac{60}{35\cdot5} \times 8 \times 9 = 121\cdot7$$

Thus, it may have been possible to increase output by 21·7 per cent by decreasing the amount of specialization. Another possibility would be to have one person carrying out operations 1 and 2 and another person carrying out operations 3, 4, 5 and 6. In this case, it might be possible to achieve the original output with only eight men,

$$\frac{60}{18\cdot9 \times 2} \times 8 \times 8 = 101\cdot6$$

However, there is not sufficient information in Fig. 15 for a final decision to be made as to the degree of specialization that is justified. Additional information would be needed on the following points.

1. The increased cost of training if the degree of specialization were reduced.

2. Whether the existing level of recruit would be suitable if the job were to change in scope.

3. Whether having less specialization would mean purchasing more equipment or allowing for changeover from one job to another.

4. Whether the operations as set out in Fig. 15 duplicated some activities and whether combining the operations would avoid such duplication. For example, operation 1 may be 'inspect' while operation 2 might be 'pack'. If the operator carried out both operations, integrating the two jobs might save lifting up and putting down.

This analysis has concentrated on the technical aspects of specialization. Human relations writers argue that too fine a specialization can also make work monotonous. Traditional management literature is apt to regard monotony as a characteristic of the job holder rather than of the job itself, though this is not always so. In 1943 Urwick wrote:

'The example of Henry Ford and his conveyor assembly work has led a good many people to exaggerate the advantages of a very minute subdivision of processes. Particularly where there is some intellectual content in the work, as for instance with clerical tasks, such minute subdivision, while it makes it possible to put almost untrained labour on to a job very quickly, also carries a number of concealed wastes. In the first place, the work makes no call on intelligence, and a worker who takes up clerical employment—indeed, all workers—usually do better where there is some demand on their intelligence and sense of responsibility. It may take a little longer to train them, but the cost is saved over and over again in accuracy and supervision. No amount of checking and inspection can overcome the proneness to error begotten of boredom.'[55]

CHAPTER III

THE HUMAN RELATIONS APPROACH

MANY social psychologists and sociologists are severe critics of the classical approach. They point out that it is people who are organized, yet the classical approach does not take into account people's likely *behaviour* under different organizational arrangements. It concentrates on their physical capacities and needs and ignores the emotional aspects of human nature. Members of an organization are viewed as passive instruments, content to act only in accordance with the rules laid down, whereas, in fact, they may pursue activities of their own which do not conform to official policy. Work groups, for example, develop their own social structure. Unless steps are taken to enlist their co-operation as an informal group, they may adopt values and practices that seriously limit the company's ability to attain its ends.

Much of the criticism is of recent origin, dating from about 1950. Before this time, research by social psychologists and sociologists was regarded as supplementary to the classical approach; conflicts tended to be ignored. Weber, a German sociologist writing at the beginning of the century, said that the most rational means for attaining an organization's prescribed goals was a 'bureaucracy'. By this he meant the large-scale organization run by specialists and professional managers emphasizing rules, records and regulations to guide conduct and decision making. Weber's ideas were developed independently and his theory of bureaucracy was part of a general theory of social and economic organization.[56] Elton Mayo's work, which initiated the human relations approach, was widely publicized by classical writers. The lack of conflict between the protagonists of human relations such as Mayo, and classical writers, exemplified by Urwick, is well illustrated by the following quotation. It is taken from Mayo's foreword to Urwick and Brech's book on the Hawthorne investigations.

'Lyndall Urwick was the first person to take public notice of the successive studies of human relations in industry undertaken by the Western Electric Company. . . . I hope that the book will be read widely by the many who are, in these days of difficulty, vitally interested in the human problems of modern industry.'[57]

There is no doubt that the classical approach is an inadequate statement of the factors to be considered in organization. The way people behave cannot be ignored any more than the behaviour of materials can be ignored when building a house. Ignoring behaviour in either case can result in failure or the revision of plans; economy of effort demands that all factors relevant to organization should be considered together.

The human relations approach is an attempt to define a social environment that stimulates people to strive for overall objectives. Hence it tries to create an organisation which

(i)   achieves objectives while satisfying its members (if organization creates dissatisfaction among the bulk of its members, it is not in a state of equilibrium),

(ii) encourages high productivity and low absenteeism,

(iii) stimulates co-operation and avoids industrial strife; it is not suggested that all minor conflicts and disagreements are to be avoided. Some disagreements ('constructive' conflicts) are inevitable and healthy; the aim is to avoid creating situations where people constantly work against each other ('destructive' conflicts).

In this approach the study of organization becomes wholly the study of behaviour; of *how* people behave and *why* they do so. Its exponents hope to predict behaviour within different organizations and to provide guidance on how best to achieve the organizational arrangements that evoke co-operation. More specifically, the approach has been concerned with the effect of organization on:

(i)   individual and group productivity,

(ii) individual development,

(iii) job satisfaction.

The study of behaviour within the business organization can be conveniently divided into:

1. Individual needs and wants.
2. Behaviour of small work groups.
3. Behaviour of supervisors.
4. Inter-group behaviour.

INDIVIDUAL NEEDS AND WANTS

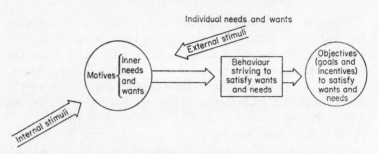

FIG. 16.—The stimulation of needs and wants leads to behaviour directed towards goals which are likely to satisfy the need or want.

The pattern of individual behaviour is illustrated in Fig. 16. Each person has certain needs and wants. When stimulated, they give rise to behaviour directed towards goals which are perceived as likely to satisfy. If people's wants and needs (i.e. their motives) were limited in number and could be identified and measured for relative importance, it might be possible to design an organization in which the employee best satisfied his needs and wants by contributing to the overall goals of the organization.

Needs and wants can only be identified indirectly. To do so requires observation of behaviour and collection of opinions. Since it is difficult to structure a situation or a questionnaire in a way that avoids all ambiguity in interpreting underlying motive, no classification of wants and needs has so far received universal acceptance. How is a strong demand for higher wages to be interpreted? Is it an attempt to satisfy the longing for security or the drive for higher social status or . . . ? We could go on indefinitely. Many motives arise purely through people's contact with the world around them and would not arise without such contact. In an atmosphere of 'keeping up with the Joneses', for example, motives are apt to change as the environment changes.

There is some agreement, however, that motives can be

classified into physiological needs and psychological wants.
Physiological needs such as hunger, thirst and sex are common
to all and develop in everyone regardless of the social environment. Psychological wants, however, appear infinite in number
and there is difficulty in demonstrating any wants that are
common to man in general. Psychologists speculate as to how
they develop. Some develop because they are associated with
the satisfaction of the physiological needs. A baby cries to be
picked up because this is associated with being fed. In whatever
way wants are acquired, they can become the basis for learning
other wants, so it becomes impossible to account fully for those
found in adults.

If it is difficult to identify and classify wants and needs, it is
even more difficult to measure their relative strengths. However,
Maier,[58] Argyris[59] and McGregor[60] have ranked them as follows:
physical, safety, social, egoistic and *self-actualization*. It is argued
that people seek to satisfy their needs in this order of priority.
As the more pressing needs are satisfied, people become concerned with self-actualization, i.e. concerned with realizing
their full potential. It follows that, in times of prosperity, an
organization which encourages narrow specialization and
emphasizes close control may prevent people from achieving
satisfaction at work, hence frustration may result. Argyris
objects to such notions as task specialization, chain of command,
span of control, on the ground that emphasis on these factors
in an organization is inconsistent with the needs and characteristics of the normal adult.

Although the above classification and ranking of needs and
wants has considerable intuitive appeal, it is still largely speculative: measuring the relative importance of wants and needs
raises problems which have not yet been solved.

Frustration

The supporters of the human relations approach claim that
many organizational arrangements give rise to frustration. The
term therefore needs to be explained. Frustration arises:

(i)   where there is a barrier to achieving some strongly-desired
      goal; it may be that the formal organization causes frustra-
      tion if it is a barrier to self-actualization;

(ii) where two wants compete with each other for satisfaction, though many such conflicts are of no significance, simply giving rise to momentary indecision.

Psychologists have classified the various types of frustration.

(i) 'Running into a stone wall.' Frustration arises if some obstacle lies in the way of achieving some highly desired goal.

(ii) 'The donkey between two bales of hay' describes the situation where a choice has to be made between equally attractive alternatives. Though this situation can lead to indecision, it is seldom frustrating since no deep anxieties are roused.

(iii) 'The devil and the deep blue sea.' In a situation where alternatives are equally distasteful, the first impulse is to run away. On this basis it is not surprising, if work is distasteful, that there should be high absenteeism and high labour turnover. The employee both hates his job and fears the consequences of not doing it.

(iv) 'Have his cake and eat it.' A worker may want more money but prefers to restrict output rather than incur the displeasure of his colleagues.

Psychologists are also concerned with classifying reactions to frustration in order that frustration may be predicted from behaviour. However, there is still no generally agreed classification though the most common reactions mentioned are aggression, rationalization, resignation, regression and sublimation.

(i) *Aggression*. The most common reaction to frustration is aggression. We hit back when frustrated though we may choose to use a scapegoat. We may even blame and hate ourselves. Industrial history is full of examples of aggressive behaviour which *may be* due to frustration. The Luddites are perhaps the most familiar. In fact, the Criminal Law Amendment Act of 1871, though repealed in 1875, was specifically directed against 'Acts of violence, intimidation, molestation and obstruction' by trade unionists.

(ii) *Rationalization* is the 'sour grapes' reaction to frustration. For example, employees whose performance is assessed on subjective factors, such as managerial attitude, may rationalize their low assessment as merely a reflection of prejudice on the part of those making the judgment.

(iii) *Resignation* arises if some frustrating situation is apathetically accepted. It reflects itself in a 'couldn't care less' attitude.

(iv) *Regression.* People may 'regress' or behave childishly in conditions of frustration, as in childish emotional outbursts and name calling from otherwise mature adults.

(v) *Sublimation* is an adaptive reaction, whereas the other reactions discussed are non-adaptive. In sublimation, frustration is removed by a transference of concentration to other goals, usually at a higher aesthetic or abstract level. Since managers cannot remove all frustration at work, they may try to get people to remove their conflicts by getting them to concentrate on other goals or by changing their minds about the importance of some of their wants.

BEHAVIOUR OF WORK GROUPS

People within a business organization do not generally behave as isolated individuals. They are either formally organized into groups or come together voluntarily and, in consequence, influence each other's behaviour. We often speak of companions having a bad or good influence. This is an overt recognition that attitudes, wants and behaviour are influenced by association with others.

The behaviour of work groups is important at every level in the organization. The human relations school claims that, in general, the behaviour of workers, supervisors and managers can be best understood and predicted through analysing the relationship among those who share some common group membership at work.

A 'group' exists when people associate with each other for some purpose. Without such a sense of common purpose and interest as a link, no group exists. Hence, the middle classes do not normally form a group unless their interests are threatened. On the other hand, a trade union is a group because its members believe that they have purposes and interests in common. The main emphasis, however, lies not in secondary groups such as trade unions but in primary groups or groups whose members have more direct contact with each other. Primary groups in practice shade off imperceptibly into secondary groups.

The early study of behaviour within work groups was carried

out at the Hawthorne (Chicago) Works of the Western Electric Company in the USA in the 1920's and early 1930's. The study was initially concerned with the effects on worker productivity of such physical factors as illumination, temperature and work schedules, but social factors, within the broad limits considered, proved more important than physical environmental factors. For example, the output of inspectors, coil winders and relay assemblers was measured under different lighting conditions. The output of the inspectors varied, but not in relation to the level of illumination. However, output from the coil winders and the relay assemblers did increase as the level of illumination was raised, but did not decrease when the level of illumination was subsequently lowered. In fact, a further study showed that merely changing the light bulbs without changing the light intensity increased output. The investigators had stumbled on to the importance of social factors in human motivation instead of discovering the relationship between physical factors and worker performance; the company had shown an interest in employee welfare and work people had responded. Social psychologists now refer to the 'Hawthorne' effect to cover those cases where the effect of direct observation in itself improves the performance of those being observed.

In order to achieve greater control, the Hawthorne investigators separated, from their regular department, a small group of workers employed in assembling telephone relays. The group was established by asking two friends to choose three other friends, The social situation fostered friendly relations among the workers and strict supervisory control was abandoned. The conditions of work, such as length of rest pauses and method of payment, were varied systematically, but productivity increased regardless of these changes. There was a possibility that the increase in output was related to changes in the financial incentive scheme. The group was being paid on its own performance whereas previously its members had been paid on the output of the whole shop consisting of a hundred operators. Two further experiments were, as a consequence, carried out to check whether it was the long-term effect of the financial incentive scheme which lay behind the increase in output. In the first experiment a second relay assembly group, again consisting of five girls, was brought together. Unlike the first assembly group, they remained in the regular shop but they were still paid in the same way, that is, on the output from their group alone. In the second of the two experiments, a third group—a mica-splitting group—was formed. This group were put into a separate room in conditions resembling those given to the first relay assembly group except that they were paid not on their own output but on the output of the shop as a whole. During the experiments the second relay assembly group increased output by 12 per cent and the mica-splitting group increased output by 15 per cent. However, since the original assembly group had increased output by 30 per cent it was argued that the original increase could not be attributed to the financial incentive alone. In fact, Roethlisberger of Harvard and Dickson of the Western Electric Company[61] are reluctant to attribute any credit for the increase in output to the financial incentive, because a number of social factors were introduced unwittingly into the experiments. The change in the wage incentive was not, therefore, the only factor that was varied. The psychologist, Viteles, makes the following comment.

'In particular, the experiments do not demonstrate that rest pauses and wages are without value as incentives to production. Furthermore, they do not justify the firm conclusion that these (or other conditions) fail to exercise independent effects upon the individual. Nevertheless, the experiments served an important purpose in calling attention to the fact that interpersonal relations and the character of the social situation can alter the effects of such specific incentives.'[62]

'Social considerations, according to the Hawthorne investigators, also outweigh economic ones in determining workers' feelings and attitudes, and thereby in determining the nature of individual satisfactions and grievances in the working situation. Objections can be raised to these generalizations, particularly to the implication that financial incentives cannot have a direct and independent influence upon output. As suggested earlier, data from the Hawthorne studies which are interpreted as revealing the effect of group sentiments can be interpreted as showing the immediate and definite influence of a change in the wage plan. Certainly, the findings of the Hawthorne studies cannot be accepted, as has apparently been done in some quarters, as demonstrating that the worker is not concerned with the size of his pay envelope except as an outer symbol of the social value of his job, and that he will ordinarily not respond directly with increased effort to an enhancement of the financial incentive.'[63]

A further important study carried out at the Hawthorne plant involved a group of fourteen experienced male operators wiring banks of relays. This group was placed in a separate room to facilitate observation. Nine of the fourteen operators wired electrical connections, three of them soldered the connections and two of them inspected the finished connections. A team was composed of three wiremen and one solderman. The group followed certain uniform patterns of behaviour which did not follow the official set-up. It restricted output in spite of the presence of a financial incentive, and rules and standards set by the Company were often replaced by those set by the group, and it was group standards (or norms) which members followed. Social factors within the group were the deciding factor in worker output and an informal organization existed; that is to say informal relations developed among workers which gave rise to organized patterns of conduct within the group. Group standards were enforced by ridicule and, if necessary, by hard blows. For example, anyone who worked too hard was a 'rate buster' or a 'speed king.' Anyone whose output was below group standard was a 'chiseler.' The group was divided into two separate cliques, though the two cliques were united in enforcing common norms. Within each clique there were differences in status. The wiremen occupied a higher status than the soldermen even though their pay was the same. The group had thus an intricate informal social structure or organization which had arisen without the intervention of management.

A good deal of work has been done subsequently on the behaviour of work groups. Any work group is more than the sum of its parts because members conform to certain standards of behaviour approved by the group. When a number of people form a group, customs develop which are regarded as an aid to the purpose at hand. No new member can associate with the group for long without adjusting his behaviour to fit. Some group standards, customs or norms, are formally accepted as rules but many remain unwritten. There are many things 'just not done' in a club which do not find expression in the rules of the club. Group members are obliged to conform to these evolved patterns of behaviour if they are to be accepted; they fall in line or get out. In practice, group customs are accepted by new members because they *want* to conform and so be accepted. Every act of each new member is strengthened or weakened (reinforced positively or negatively) depending on the extent to which other group members indicate approval or disapproval.

Arthur Koestler described in *The Observer* (February 10, 1963) his initiation into the ways of a work group:

'I learned to conform to our unwritten Rules of Life: Go slow; it's a mug's game anyway; if you play it, you are letting your mates down; if you seek betterment, promotion, you are breaking ranks and will be sent to Coventry. My comrades could be lively and full of bounce; at the working site they moved like figures in a slow-motion film, or deep-sea divers on the ocean bed.

'The most cherished rituals of our tribal life were the tea-and-bun-breaks—serene, protracted, like a Japanese tea ceremony. Another fascinating tribal custom was the punctuation of every sentence with four letter-words used, as adjectives, without reference to meaning, compulsive like hiccoughs. It was not swearing, these strings of dehydrated obscenity served as a kind of negative status symbol.'

Violence can be still used to ensure conformity: 'A guardsman yesterday told officers of an alleged two hour "punch-up" he received for letting the side down by going to bed with a dirty face.'

Even a strong and dominant personality must conform to some extent and gauge how far he can go at any one time in modifying the accepted codes of behaviour. Work groups usually develop norms on such matters as what constitutes a fair day's pay and other working conditions. It is foolish to ignore such norms or to dismiss them as mere prejudice. It is common sense to try to get work groups to go along with change through understanding their perceptions rather than giving them the impression of being pushed around. As one writer says, 'Much pegging of output at a certain level by employees is an expression of this need to protect their ways of life as well as their livelihood from too rapid change.'

As an example of the way a work group can vitiate manage-

F

ment plans, is the case described by Selekman. Five workers in a clothing plant were required by management to sew only one section each of a coat whereas previously they had worked as a team and completed sewing the five sections together. The aim by management in making the change was to put each man on individual bonus. However, the five men, though of different abilities, continued to share the bonus.[64]

Are work group norms ever conducive to the achievement of management goals? Fortunately, a work group may identify its interests with those who formed it so that informal and formal goals coincide. What if goals do not coincide? Can psychologists suggest some means for reconciling the two? The main method so far developed is to involve work groups in decisions that directly affect them. This will be discussed later.

THE 'MAJORITY' EFFECT

The tendency to conform to group pressures is stronger than most people suspect. Group members are prepared on occasions to see black as white if their colleagues argue that way. One psychologist, Asch, devised an experiment in which subjects were invited to match the length of a given line with one of three unequal lines. The task was easy and participants left alone found it so. However, when a subject found himself in the company of others who, like himself, had to voice their opinions aloud, but had also been instructed to agree on a judgment which was clearly wrong, there was a strong tendency for the odd man out to fall in line with the majority opinion. This 'majority effect' is even more marked in circumstances where the discrimination is difficult though a subject is less likely to conform if he has supporters.[65]

A business, like a group, can demand a high degree of conformity and loyalty from its executives with undesirable side-effects on individual creativity, as pointed out by W. H. Whyte in his famous book *The Organisation Man*.[66] The community, too, can make demands. Riesman suggests that in American suburbia there is high pressure on a child to behave as other children, and this comes not only from other children but also from parents and teachers. Parents worry if a child is the odd one out even if his behaviour is in no way criminal. He claims that in America there is an admiration for the man who can influence people, but scepticism towards accepted belief is not encouraged. As a consequence, creativity is not encouraged as this presupposes uneasiness about the existing state of affairs.[67]

PROBLEM SOLVING IN GROUPS

In spite of what has been said, two heads are often better than one. Where the solution to a problem is a matter of logic or knowledge, then a large group is likely to contain some expert whose confidence wins over the rest. In fact, even the views of the expert might be improved by the opinions of the laymen. There have been a number of experiments in which people in groups give a collective solution which is better than any individual solution. Most problems, however, considered in these experiments led to solutions which did not conflict with group aims. If a possible solution to a problem does, in practice, conflict with certain group attitudes, an individual may be inhibited and hesitate to make his colleagues face realities.

LEADERSHIP IN GROUPS

If a person exercises influence over colleagues much more than they do over him, he is said to exercise leadership. If this influence covers a wide range, he is described as a leader. It is commonplace to view a leader as possessing a combination of personality traits so that we speak of choosing 'natural leaders' and attempt to list their supposed qualities. The position in practice is more complex. Whether leadership is provided to a group depends not only on personal characteristics but on the situation in which the group finds itself. The communist who is normally ridiculed may be the chosen leader during a strike if there is a feeling that he will not compromise in negotiation. Hence, leaders in one situation may be unacceptable in another. The positions of Chamberlain in 1939 and Churchill in 1945 will readily come to mind.

The work group leader is likely to be the person whose activities most coincide with group norms, that is, the man whose behaviour is perceived as most likely to achieve group needs. This concept of leadership has serious implications. The leader cannot deviate too quickly from the expected pattern of behaviour, though, if he rates high in carrying out the main rules, his infringement of minor ones may be overlooked. An attempt to win over the leader, even if successful, does not ensure winning over the group. Social psychologists emphasize that managements are not dealing with a 'rabble' but with 'well-knit work groups'. Hence, it may be more effective to deal with a small group as a whole than to deal separately with individual group members. Groups can be persuaded to change together, whereas the single member may close his mind to argument if a change in his behaviour implies facing group disapproval.

ATTITUDES AND MORALE

Wants and needs, when aroused, influence behaviour. However, the particular want or need aroused results not so much from the stimulus itself as from the way the stimulus is experienced. The manager and worker may experience the same situation in different ways. A new machine may be regarded by the manager simply as a means for reducing costs, while the worker may regard it as a threat to his economic security and react accordingly.

The way in which a stimulus is experienced depends on attitudes which are usually developed through group membership, as groups tend to control attitudes by the same mechanism as they enforce other norms. In practice both attitudes and motives interact upon each other. An attitude is usually defined as a state of readiness to respond in a certain way to a particular type of situation. From the thousands of different ways of responding to various situations, there are some uniformities or acquired predispositions to react in certain ways to some particular object, situation or person. These predispositions are based on the attitudes held. From a knowledge of attitudes it may be possible to predict opinions or reactions to some point at issue; conversely, attitudes are gauged by examining opinions and reactions. If we know that a group has a suspicious attitude to management, it would not be hard to predict its likely reaction to the suggested introduction of work measurement. Attitudes so strong as to make the individual ignore the evidence are called prejudices. People are not always aware of their prejudices; this was indicated by an experiment in which students ranked sixteen pieces of prose in order of merit. The passages had all been written by Stevenson but were attributed to a variety of authors whom the students had already ranked in order of merit. The ranking of authors and the rankings of the pieces of prose attributed to them were highly correlated.[68]

Management is obviously interested in creating 'right attitudes' to facilitate changes of behaviour. Since the normal communication between worker and management gives too crude a measure of existing attitudes, there has been a growth of more direct means of measurement. Unfortunately, much social psychology today is concerned with collecting information about attitudes; consequently, fundamental work on organizational behaviour (such as the Hawthorne experiment) is rare.

The crudest measure of attitude would be simply to count up the number of people for or against some particular view. This, however, would merely measure the direction of attitude whereas for deeper understanding it is also necessary to measure both the extremeness of the attitude and the intensity of feeling involved. Sometimes the salience of the attitude is also measured, i.e. whether the attitude occupies a major or minor position in the total scale of attitudes held. The attitude towards war is likely to have a higher ranking relative to other attitudes than it did before World War II.

There are a number of ways of evolving an attitude scale in order to describe and rank people's attitudes. By one method, after the particular attitude has been defined (for example attitude towards payment by results) several hundred statements on the subject are collected. A large number of judges (50 to 300) working independently rank these statements into eleven groups, ranging from an extremely unfavourable attitude to an extremely favourable attitude towards the subject. The sixth position is regarded as neutral, reflecting neither favourableness nor unfavourableness. Those statements giving rise to ambiguity in ranking are discarded.

The remaining statements are given a scale value ranging from (say) zero to ten. A final selection is made from the statements to cover the scale from one extreme position to the other.

Example

Scale Value

10   1. I think this company treats its employees better than another company.

8.5 2. If I were starting again I would still join this company.

etc.

Note: Scale values not shown on questionnaire.

The employee marks all statements with which he agrees and his 'attitude score' on the subject is the average of all score values he has marked. It should be noted that, since attitude is an 'intensive' quality like 'softness', it is meaningless to say that one man's attitude is 50 per cent higher than another man's if he obtains a score of nine as against six. Also, identical scores by this method of measurement may reflect different attitudinal patterns since identical average scores can arise from marking off radically different statements.

The measurement of morale is similar to the measurement of attitudes, morale being one reflection of attitudes. Although morale can be defined in terms of job satisfaction, there is growing agreement that the term be reserved to cover team spirit. On this definition, it is possible for each member of a work group to be highly motivated but for morale, or team spirit, to be low. High morale can sometimes work against the formal organization; high morale in some prisoner-of-war camps did not help the guards. Similarly, morale may be high during a strike. Where group purposes and organization objectives are made to coincide, high morale, by fostering a co-operative spirit, helps to achieve an integrated effort. The fact that industrial situations today frequently demand close co-operation is a further reason in favour of stimulating morale.

The measurement of attitudes and morale is still crude. What people say they do and what they actually do are often very different, and yet attitude measurement attempts to measure people's predisposition to *act* in a certain way. Even when questionnaires are unambiguous, contain no leading questions or emotive language and the sampling of items on the questionnaire is adequate, there is still the problem of whether people give truthful replies. No amount of statistical juggling can eliminate the factor of dishonest replies and the unconscious bias of interviewers. There is only one way of writing 'no', but many ways of saying it. Viteles illustrates this possibility of bias by quoting an investigation by Rice into the recorded interviews made by twelve trained and conscientious interviewers among 2,000 homeless. Rice found that one interviewer who was an ardent prohibitionist had attributed the downfall of 62 per cent of those interviewed to alcohol and 7 per cent due to industrial conditions. A socialist interviewer found alcohol was the reason in only 22 per cent of cases and 39 had been the result of industrial conditions; whilst the prohibitionist stated that 34 per cent of the homeless had themselves given alcohol as the cause of their downfall, the socialist quoted only 11 per cent as giving alcohol as the reason.[69]

Obviously, tests of the reliability and validity of each attitude survey are essential if they are to be used to predict behaviour rather than to describe collective opinion. A test of reliability is concerned with the consistency of answers. When groups are tested and then re-tested the degree of correlation between answers indicates reliability, that is, reliability means that comparable but independent measures of the same attitude should give similar results. Tests on validity are concerned with ensuring that differences in scores reflect true differences among individuals in the characteristics being measured so that the survey measures what it sets out to measure, i.e. a predisposition to react in a particular way to a given situation. Some tests of validity have been merely concerned with ensuring consistency in interpreting the underlying attitude behind answers given. This is insufficient. The findings of an attitude survey should be used to predict and its validity should be established by demonstrating that the predictions are adequate. This is the counsel of perfection as there are many practical difficulties involved. One is the same as that encountered in the measurement of motives.

People may not attempt to satisfy one deep want because it is incompatible with satisfying some even deeper want. Where there is a multiplicity of wants, the satisfaction of one may mean not satisfying others. In the Hawthorne experiment, individuals in the bank wiring group preferred to stay true to group norms than to earn more money by increasing output. Hence, a survey may detect an attitude, but that attitude may not reflect itself in behaviour because other factors in the situation may inhibit it. Some attitudes, as a consequence, may never get beyond stated opinion.

There are a number of more indirect ways of determining attitudes than those discussed. All, however, are difficult to test for validity. As Selltiz, Jahoda, Deutsch and Cook point out:

'As we indicated earlier, many questions have been raised about the validity of indirect techniques, and relatively little research evidence is available to answer them. Actually, as noted in the preceding chapter, there is not much evidence of the validity of direct techniques depending on self-report, such as interviews and questionnaires. The validity of such instruments is less often questioned, however, probably because of the 'obvious' relevance of the questions to the characteristics they are intended to measure. It is the degree of inference involved in indirect tests—the gap between the subject's response and the characteristic it is presumed to indicate—that intensifies questions about validity.'[70]

MEASURING GROUP DIMENSIONS

Questionnaires have been designed to compare and describe the internal relations of work groups as a basis for predicting behaviour. For example, they have been designed to describe groups along the following dimensions:

Intimacy: Degree to which members are acquainted with each other.

Homogeneity: Degree to which members resemble each other in background of age, sex, attitudes.

Hedonic Tone: Degree to which members find pleasure in membership of group.

Autonomy: Degree to which group is independent of other groups.

Control: Degree to which group regulates behaviour of members.

Flexibility: Degree to which procedures are laid down.

Stratification: Degree to which members' status is defined.

Permeability: Degree or ease to which new members are admitted.

Polarisation: Degree to which members are orientated towards specific goals.

Cohesiveness: Degree to which means of achieving goals are shared or the extent to which the group functions as a unit.[71]

For example, a group high in morale would be high in cohesiveness, participation and stability.

Another technique used to describe the internal relationships of groups is the sociogram. Each member of a group indicates his acceptance or rejection of other members according to some given clear-cut criterion. Where a questionnaire is used, care has to be taken to make sure the criterion is unambiguous.

In an office reorganization (by the author) nine clerks were formed into three teams of three to achieve a better manning on sections and to ensure that at least one clerk in each team was available to answer telephoned queries from customers. Each clerk was asked to choose three others with whom he would like to work. The resulting sociogram is shown in Fig. 17. 'A' is called a 'star' and 'I' an 'isolate'. In fact, 'I', in spite of specific instructions to nominate three others, only chose two. From this sociogram each member's sociometric score can be calculated by adding up the number of occasions he was chosen.

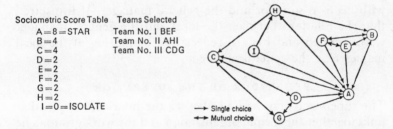

Sociometric Score Table	Teams Selected
A=8=STAR	Team No. I BEF
B=4	Team No. II AHI
C=4	Team No. III CDG
D=2	
E=2	
F=2	
G=2	
H=2	
I=0=ISOLATE	

⟶ Single choice
⟷ Mutual choice

FIG. 17.—Sociogram showing the preferences when members were asked to nominate three other group members with whom they would like to work. 'A' is the informal group leader.

The sociogram was used to choose the three teams and these are also shown in Fig. 17. The presence of star 'A' in team AHI raised its prestige from what would otherwise have been a very low level. 'A' also, in growing closer to 'H' and 'I', had the effect of getting them integrated with the rest of the group. The sociogram shows the high position of influence held by 'A', which is a factor making for group cohesiveness in spite of the closeness of clique BEF.

In the same case, three supervisors P, Q, R, were asked to say with which superior they had most business contact. The dotted line in Fig. 18 indicates their answers. R claimed he had most dealings with the general manager to whom his own superior reported, while Q insisted he had equal dealings both

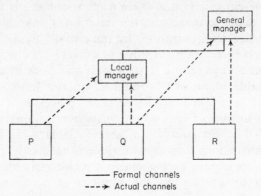

FIG. 18.—Sociogram showing the formal and informal communications net between supervisors and managers.

with his own superior and the general manager. It transpired that the relations between the local and the general manager were strained and Fig. 18 reflects the by-passing of the local manager by the general manager.

BEHAVIOUR OF THE SUPERVISOR

The supervisor may be described as the interlocking pin that links together the formal organization and the work group. The human relations school regards the attitudes and behaviour of the supervisor as a major factor in influencing work group behaviour; more specifically, as a major factor in determining group productivity and job satisfaction. All the recommend-ations as to 'ideal' supervisory behaviour lead to what has been called 'power equalization', that is, to reducing the differences in power and status between supervisor and subordinate.

How should the supervisor behave, or in fact how should any superior behave, to those beneath him if he is to achieve high productivity? Remember that leadership is not now evaluated purely in terms of a stereotyped list of personality traits but in terms of the behaviour that is effective in influencing others in the given situation. There are, of course, innumerable specific behaviours exhibited by supervisors but these can be classified into a limited number of groups, the behaviours within each group being identical from the point of view of their effect on subordinates. Although there is no one supervisory pattern of behaviour which under all circumstances is most effective, it is claimed that employee-centred rather than job-centred, democratic rather than authoritative supervisory behaviour, is more likely to achieve high productivity and job satisfaction.

EMPLOYEE-CENTRED VERSUS JOB-CENTRED SUPERVISION

Rensis Likert of Michigan University distinguishes between employee-centred and job-centred supervision.[72] The employee-centred supervisor:

(i)   Is considerate but firm and acts in a way that emphasises personal worth. He has a genuine interest in the success and well-being of subordinates.

(ii) Does not interfere but is supportive.

(iii) Has confidence in his subordinates and therefore his expectations are high. He sets high goals but leaves his subordinates to get on with the job.

(iv) Develops high group loyalty and uses participative techniques.

The job-centred supervisor channels his attention on the job to be done and is apt to regard employees merely as instruments for achieving production goals. He gives close supervision and delegates as few decisions as possible.

Likert argues that, in general, employee-centred supervisors

FIG. 19.—Consideration and Initiating Structure as co-ordinate, independent axes. Supervisor A is about average on both dimensions. Supervisor D is high on Consideration and Structure behaviour. Supervisor C is high on Consideration and average on Structure. Supervisor B has a pattern which many would call 'authoritarian'. Supervisor E appears to operate in a *laissez-faire* manner and may not be exerting much 'leadership'. A particular supervisor's relative standing on these dimensions may be measured by means of a questionnaire. (Reprinted by permission from Gagné and Fleishman, *Psychology and Human Performance*, copyright (c) 1959 by Holt, Rinehart & Winston, Inc., New York.)

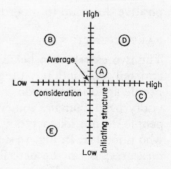

achieve the higher productivity. A supervisor will not give leadership to his work group unless he helps them to achieve their goals, which postulates his being employee-centred.

A similar conclusion to Likert's is taken by Fleishman, who claims that the ideal supervisory behaviour from the point of view of getting the best out of subordinates is that which emphasizes consideration and also gives a firm lead.[73] Fig. 19 illustrates the position. Supervisory behaviour should be positive in both consideration and initiating structure (giving a definite lead) though the exact position will vary with the situation.

Consideration

(i)   He sees that a person is rewarded for a job well done,
(ii) He makes people feel at ease when with him,
(iii) He backs his men,
(iv) He discusses proposed changes with his subordinates if the changes affect them,

and so on.

Giving a firm lead

(i)   He criticises bad work,
(ii) he encourages people to make greater efforts,
(iii) he offers new approaches to problems,

and so on.

The essential point to note is that the two patterns of behaviour are independent of each other. Contrary to popular belief, it is possible to be considerate and at the same time to give positive direction to subordinates.

PARTICIPATION

The two extremes in behaviour are *autocratic* (treat 'em rough and tell 'em nothing) ranging through to *laissez-faire*, where people are allowed to do as they like. The most efficient supervisory behaviour lies somewhere between these two extremes: people do not like a tyrant, but neither do they like someone who is too lax. In Fig. 19 supervisor A is about average on both measures; B can be described as authoritarian; C is high in consideration and average on structure; D is high on both consideration and structure, while E can be described *laissez-faire.* There appears to be general agreement that the *laissez-faire* pattern gets less out of subordinates than any other supervisory behaviour.

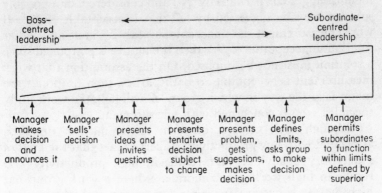

FIG. 20.—Continuum of leadership behaviour. (from *Leadership Organization* by Tannenbaum, Weschler and Massarik, copyright © 1961, used by permission of McGraw-Hill Book Company).

Fig. 20, showing a range in supervisory behaviour from authoritarian to extremely democratic, indicates that the essential difference between the two ends of the range lies in the degree of authority used by the superior and the amount of freedom in decision-making given to subordinates. Under democratic leadership, subordinates participate in decisions that affect them but are not allowed to do just what they like as under *laissez-faire* leadership. It is claimed that democratic leadership is more effective in getting high performance because it achieves personal commitment to decisions made collectively, and encourages individual creativity. Furthermore, where work groups participate, then group pressure brings about overall commitment of the group. Where several levels are involved, it is preferable to give the lowest levels an early opportunity to participate if participation is not to appear illusory.

In general, the human relations school is concerned with achieving work group participation in the decision-making process. Full work group participation might be carried out as follows:

Assume 'A' wishes to get work group 'Z' to accept (say) work measurement. Group 'Z' are called together and perceive through discussion the management problem in work scheduling, etc. Also through discussion, work group 'Z' takes on the task of considering a solution. Various suggestions are made by 'Z' and 'A' points out their drawbacks, if any. Work measurement is suggested (perhaps by 'A') and considered, or a possible solution may be suggested by 'Z' that is acceptable to 'A'. If work measurement is unacceptable to 'Z' and any other solution unacceptable to 'A', then the matter is postponed since a solution must not be imposed. On the assumption that work measurement is acceptable to both parties, then proposals are made as to the way in which group 'Z' will help the work study specialist who is concerned with measurement.

Although high morale (or team spirit) may at times be associated with low productivity, Likert argues that the kind of supervisory behaviour that results in high productivity also results in high work group morale. Where a work group has high morale it has greater control over its members and such control is exercised to achieve group goals. Management can never control as effectively as the group since 'it is in almost constant contact with all its members and maintains an all-seeing surveillance of their activities; the informal group is self-policing and can relieve management of much of the burden of supervision when the group is co-operatively oriented.' Where democratic leadership is exercised there is a greater likelihood that group goals and company objectives will coincide.

Does employee participation in decision-making reduce the influence exerted by the supervisor? Likert does not think so. He argues that when superiors have the sole authority for making decisions, they exert more influence on the decision-making itself but exert less influence on what actually goes on than when subordinates participate in decisions.

EVIDENCE

The most famous study indicating that people behave differently under different patterns of supervisory leadership was conducted by two psychologists, White and Lippitt.[74] The investigation was concerned with four groups of children each containing five boys formed into 'clubs' built around the recreational activities of aeroplane model construction and similar hobbies. The boys in each group were matched with regard to background. Four group leaders were trained to act as democratic, authoritarian and *laissez-faire* leaders. As autocrats, the group leaders just told the children what to do and kept the group working. As democrats, the leaders were considerate and, although they gave a lead and help, they encouraged the group to decide issues as a group and to allocate work among themselves. As *laissez-faire* leaders, they simply indicated that they were available if wanted and then left the group to get on with the job. The group leaders moved from group to group at the same time changing their leadership pattern. The results are of interest. Under autocratic leadership, output was highest, but only when the leader was present. The group showed little initiative and was unimaginative. In addition, team spirit was low. *Laissez-faire* leadership gave the poorest results, output being both low and unimaginative. Under democratic leadership both morale and the quality of work was highest but output was slightly lower than under autocratic leadership.

The best-known work on supervisory behaviour in business was carried out by the Institute for Social Research whose Director is Rensis Likert. In one illustrative case, low-producing sections at the Prudential Insurance Company in the USA were compared with high-producing ones.[75] As the sections were subject to the same working conditions and company policies, differences in output were assumed to be either due to the quality of management and supervision or to the social relations within the groups. A study was undertaken to test whether supervisory and management behaviour affected productivity through first of all affecting morale. The attitudes of worker and supervisor were measured and related to sectional efficiency. The analysis suggested that supervisors of high-producing sections tended to exhibit the employee-centred behaviour. A further study was carried out on maintenance-of-way groups on the railways. The findings were similar, except that the Prudential investigation found that high-producing supervisors exercised only general rather than close supervision of subordinates, whereas this was not confirmed in the second study. It appears that where the job to be done is simple relative to ability, close supervision is undesirable. On the other hand, where the job is non-routine, close guidance is welcome. In neither study did relations between group members account for differences in productivity.

The study was based on survey data rather than direct

experimentation. However, Likert does quote one field experiment carried out at the insurance company by the Institute for Social Research. This study covered 500 clerical employees in four parallel divisions. Unfortunately, it was not conclusive. In fact, groups subjected to the more authoritative behaviour had a slightly higher productivity. Likert points out that adverse employee attitudes were developed in the group subject to the more authoritative behaviour. In the long run, he argues, if the experiment had continued, the difference in attitudes between the democratic and the authoritative would have made themselves felt so that the democratic group would have been more productive, since all other evidence points to this.

Likert comments as follows:

'Apparently, the hierarchically controlled program, at the end of one year, was in a state of unstable equilibrium. Although productivity was then high, forces were being created, as the measures of the intervening variables and turnover indicated, which subsequently would adversely affect the high level of productivity. Good people were leaving the organization because of feeling "too much pressure on them to produce". Hostility towards high producers and towards supervision, decreased confidence and trust in management, these and similar attitudes were being developed. Such attitudes create counterforces to management's pressure for high productivity. These developments would gradually cause the productivity level to become lower.'[76]

This argument is not impressive, Likert conducts an experiment because he recognizes the weakness of existing evidence; attitude survey data leaves many questions unanswered as to cause. Likert, however, interprets the results of the experiment in a way that presupposes that the existing evidence is already conclusive. Also a point which appears to have been treated lightly is the small differences investigated which were around 5 per cent. Such differences could be explained by the crudeness of the measurements of productivity between sections and through differences in work methods and quality standards, differences which could only have been revealed by a detailed method study. However, the evidence does indicate that democratic and employee-centred supervisory behaviour is as effective, if not better, than any other pattern of behaviour.

As democratic behaviour may also lead to more adjusted subordinates, it is to be recommended.

All participative techniques for gaining co-operation owe most to Kurt Lewin and the School of Field Theory he founded. He also founded the Research Centre for Group Dynamics at the Massachusetts Institute of Technology which is now under Likert at Michigan. The Group Dynamics movement has been responsible for developing most of the laboratory techniques for studying small groups. Some of Lewin's experiments demonstrate how attitudes and behaviour can be changed by participation. For example, during World War II, an attempt was made to change the way housewives were using meat. An expert lectured a group of women on the subject but only 3 per cent experimented with the suggested meats. In another group of like background, a discussion leader led the women in discussing the subject among themselves, and all participated in formulating conclusions. A follow-up showed that 32 per cent of the women had tried the foods previously rejected.[77]

One industrial experiment was carried out at the Harwood Manufacturing Company in Virginia, usa, by Lewin and some of his followers, Bavelas, French and Coch. A problem facing management was resistance to job changes, frequently accompanied by a drop in output. At the time of the experiment several minor but comparable job changes were needed. One group affected by these changes was selected as the *control* group and so given the usual treatment. When changes were introduced the production department changed the job and set a new piece rate, then the workers in the group were called together and told that the change was necessary because of competitive conditions and the new piece rate was explained. After questions had been answered, all the control group returned to work.

Changes were also introduced in work being carried out by three other groups called the *experimental* groups. Before any changes were made, the supervisor called together those affected. The problem was explained to the group and was discussed by them. A number of suggestions were made and the group agreed that savings could be made by eliminating 'frills'; they agreed that a method study specialist should analyse the work and that they would try any new methods suggested. The groups were also given the opportunity to participate in proposed changes. One group participated in changes by having group representatives act on their behalf, but all members in the other two groups participated in planning job modifications. There was a dramatic difference in results between the control and experimental groups. The production of the control group actually dropped and output had still not recovered at the end of the forty-day trial period. There was also considerable resentment about the new piece rate, though later examination showed this to be more loose than tight. In the two groups where full participation was used, output increased in the forty-day experimental period to a level that was about 14 per cent higher than the group had ever previously attained. The new piece rate was accepted and there were no signs of frustrated behaviour. The group which participated through representation increased output but by less than 14 per cent.

Also at Harwood another experiment was carried out by Bavelas in which small groups of workers (four to twelve workers in each group) were brought together under a leader who led a discussion on the advantage of team work. The leader put it to the group that they might like to set higher output goals for themselves and each group eventually agreed. As a result, output from these groups was increased by around 18 per cent, whereas output remained the same for other matched groups who were not involved in these discussions.

Viteles comments on the Harwood experiments as follows:

'The design for neither study, as reported by the investigators, eliminated the possibility that variables other than participation in decision-making played a role in accounting for the production differences between the *control* and the *experimental* groups.

'Of special importance, in the first of these studies, is an apparent difference in the character of the training received by operators in the two groups. While none of the available reports on this study are particularly clear with respect to this issue, it quite definitely appears that more and better training was received by members of the *experimental* groups than by members of the *control* groups. In the second study, as reported by French, it seems quite evident that each of the experimental groups was supplied with considerable *knowledge of results*, in the form of graphs showing changes in the productivity of the group. There is no indication that similar information was supplied to the *control* groups. . . . Failure to control adequately the possible effects of difference in training, in knowledge of results (and possibly of other variables) makes it impossible to accept the view that the increased output by the *experimental* groups in the Harwood plant studies was necessarily due *solely* to employee participation in decision-making. Nevertheless, the general nature of the experiments and of findings from these and other studies still support the view that employee participation in decision-making can contribute to increased employee productivity.'[78]

CRITICISM OF GROUP PARTICIPATION

Group participation in decision-making in the way described has been criticized on a number of grounds.

(i) Group participation gives the work group more power over its members. This may lead to a tyranny which is far worse than the autocracy of management.

(ii) It may result in decisions that run counter to the best judgment of experts. No adequate explanation has been given as to why participation should necessarily lead subordinates into adopting organization goals as their own.

(iii) It blurs responsibilities and individual accountability for performance.

(iv) It may lead to greater motivation and morale but not to greater productivity as the existing technology may set an upper limit to this.

(v) The gains from participation may be far less than the cost of changing supervisory patterns of behaviour and the cost of time consumed in committee.

(vi) Group participation may be ineffective unless supervisors and managers have the right attitudes; true participation cannot be imposed but must evolve naturally from the attitudes and values held by supervisors and managers. These may need to be changed through counselling. The emphasis here is placed on changing people rather than changing procedures or organization structures. Thus Argyris argues 'The development of skills without appropriate changes in values becomes, at best, an alteration whose lack of depth and manipulative character will become easily evident to others. Skills follow values; values rarely follow skills.'[79]

(vii) Strauss, of the University of California, Berkeley, stresses the current weaknesses in research. 'Considering the rather limited amount of research done, there is too much loose talk about the "proven" superiority of group-decision and participative methods. The studies cited chiefly involved women in war-time (food change), partially industrialized mountain folk (Harwood), and undergraduate students in psychology. Further research should involve various kinds of groups, various types of tasks, and various forms of participation.'[80]

THEORY 'X' AND THEORY 'Y'

Sometimes the results of a series of different experiments can be brought together and shown to be simply applications of a more general rule. This more general rule is called a 'theory'. McGregor of Massachusetts Institute of Technology makes a distinction between what he terms Theory X and Theory Y.[81] Both theories represent different views as to man's nature.

Theory X assumes that:

1. The average man is by nature indolent—he works as little as possible.

2. He lacks ambition, dislikes responsibility, prefers to be led.

3. He is inherently self-centred, indifferent to organizational needs.

4. He is by nature resistant to change.

5. He is gullible, not very bright, the ready dupe of the charlatan and the demagogue.[82]

Behind Theory Y is the view that:

1. People are not by nature passive or resistant to organizational needs. They have become so as a result of experience in organization.

2. The motivation, the potential for development, the capacity for assuming responsibility, the readiness to direct behaviour towards organizational goals are all present in people. Management does not put them there. It is a responsibility of management to make it possible for people to recognize and develop these human characteristics for themselves.

3. The essential task of management is to arrange organizational conditions and methods of operation so that people can
achieve their own goals best by directing their own efforts
towards organizational objectives.[83]

A number of recommendations made by McGregor and
others rest on the assumption that people are not inherently
indolent and so on, but became so through their treatment.

'The social scientist does not deny that human behaviour in
industrial organization today is approximately what management perceives it to be. He has, in fact, observed it and studied
it fairly extensively. But he is pretty sure that this behaviour is
not a consequence of man's inherent nature. It is a consequence
rather of the nature of industrial organizations, of management
philosophy, policy, and practice. The conventional approach
of Theory X is based on mistaken notions of what is cause and
what is effect.'[84]

McGregor in this passage implies that people's conduct must
either be the cause or the effect of classical management
policies. This is a fallacy. Both management practices and
people's behaviour can modify and affect each other. Mental
illness can cause physical illness; but physical illness can also
cause mental illness.

INTER-GROUP BEHAVIOUR

Every business organization is composed of a number of work
groups. Inter-group behaviour is concerned with the relations
between these groups as they are a factor in achieving overall
company objectives; a high level of achievement may require
a high level of co-operation and co-ordination among groups.
A famous study on inter-group behaviour was that carried
out by W. F. Whyte in 1944.[85] He studied inter-group relations
in a restaurant and found that where lower status workers,
such as waitresses, made direct demands on higher status
workers, such as cooks, then conflict resulted and efficiency was
lowered. Whyte concluded that the normal flow of demands in
inter-group relations should not flow from lower to higher status
groups but vice versa if conflict is to be reduced. Thus cooks did
not expect to be given orders by waitresses. Conflict was reduced
when an impersonal barrier, namely a spindle on which wait-

resses placed their food orders, was erected between cooks and waitresses.

A further study of interest was made by Sherif.[86] He found that conflict among groups could be reduced by introducing 'superordinate' goals, that is to say goals desired by the two or more groups in conflict but which cannot be achieved except by the combined efforts of all.

The conclusions from both the above studies have considerable intuitive appeal. Different groups need shared values and goals if they are to co-operate. A conflict between sales and production may arise because the two feel no strong sense of common purpose. It is also a matter of common observation that where demands flow contrary to status lines—from lower status to higher status groups—conflict arises unless steps are taken to avoid it by:

(i) Creating intermediary groups to act in a liaison capacity, such as production planning between sales and production or product planning between Sales and Research Development. In both these cases, the difference in status may be imaginary, each department believing itself the superior one.

(ii) Allocating a low-status member of the high-status group to deal with the low-status group (the shop steward has to see the foreman, not the manager).

(iii) Indicating that the lower status member is acting on behalf of a high-status member. A young specialist demanding information in a department may be resented unless it is made clear that he is acting on behalf of higher management.

HUMAN RELATIONS AND CLASSICAL ORGANIZATION PROBLEMS

GROUPING INTO SECTIONS AND HIGHER ADMINISTRATIVE UNITS

Flat versus Pyramidal Structure

The human relations school stresses the importance of minimizing the number of vertical levels in an organization. A flat structure as opposed to a pyramid structure is recommended (Fig. 21).

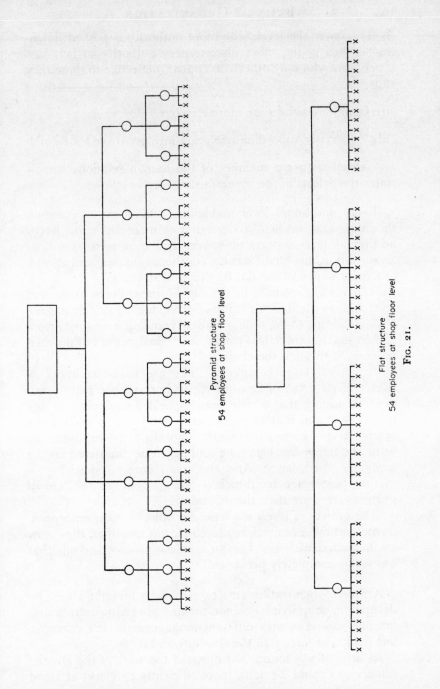

Pyramid structure
54 employees at shop floor level

Flat structure
54 employees at shop floor level

Fig. 21.

(i) The fewer the levels, the more authority is pushed downwards, thus giving more discretionary authority to first line supervisors who may otherwise appear ineffective to those they supervise.

(ii) Communications are more effective.

(iii) Supervisor/subordinate relationships need to be less formal.

(iv) Drucker (not a member of the human relations school) states the defects of the pyramid structure as follows:

'Every additional level makes the attainment of common direction and mutual understanding more difficult. Every additional level distorts objectives and misdirects attention. Every link in the chain sets up additional stresses, and creates one more source of inertia, friction and slack.

'Above all, especially in the big business, every additional level adds to the difficulty of developing tomorrow's managers, both by adding to the time it takes to come up from the bottom and by making specialists rather than managers out of the men moving up through the chain.

'In several large companies there are today as many as twelve levels between first-line supervisor and company president. Assuming that a man gets appointed supervisor at age twenty-five, and that he spends only five years on each intervening level—both exceedingly optimistic assumptions—he would be eighty-five before he could even be considered for the company's presidency. And the usual cure—a special promotion ladder for hand-picked young 'geniuses' or 'crown princes'—is worse than the disease.

'The growth of levels is a serious problem for any enterprise, no matter how organized. For levels are like tree rings; they grow by themselves with age. It is an insidious process, and one that cannot be completely prevented.'[87]

A flatter organization structure may be brought about by delegation, simplifying decision-making, de-centralization and forming sub-units with different managements. For example, one field sales force had the structure in Fig. 22.

In brief, it was found that much of the work of the District Supervisors could be done more efficiently by clerks at Head

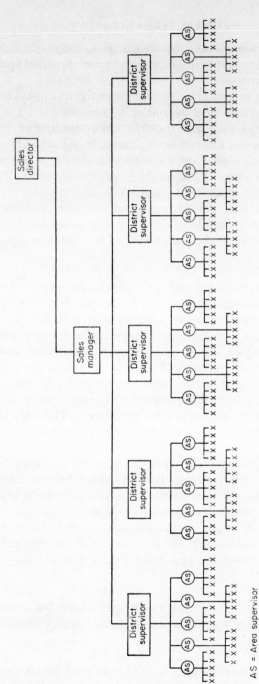

AS = Area supervisor
X = Salesman

FIG. 22.

Office. Other work could be passed on to Area Supervisors, if policy was more explicitly stated, and more decisions could be made by the salesmen.

After the investigation, a reason given for still justifying the District Supervisor level was that it created greater opportunities for promotion and thus the more able salesmen were retained. However, the increased promotion opportunity meant that the good salesmen were lost anyway as they were promoted. Promotion, too, must have led to much disappointment since so much of the managerial work was of a routine clerical nature. In addition, selling costs were excessive and the very existence of levels made everyone promotion-conscious in a desire to be closer to the man who had the ultimate say.

Sectional Over-specialization

In the same way that high-task specialization can narrow the man, the human scientist argues that it is also possible for a department or section to over-specialize so that its contribution to overall company goals becomes blurred. In such circumstances, sectional or departmental goals may be at variance with the best interests of the company. Fig. 23(a) illustrates the position. The figure shows three departments each divided into three sections. Each section is carrying out identical work, as illustrated by the similarity of letters in the boxes. There is a strong need for co-ordination if each department is not to go its own way.

An alternative organizational arrangement is shown in Fig. 23(b) where each department is independent, being made up of each of the three different types of sections. Such an organizational arrangement may achieve a better integration of the three distinct activities, but it may also lead to losses arising through activities being carried out on a smaller scale or through there being less opportunity for specialization.

Choice of Supervisor

The importance of choosing supervisors who allow participation and are employee-centred has already been discussed.

Choice of Team Members

Sociometric methods have been used to fit work teams together. One case has already been quoted. One published study involved seventy-two carpenters and bricklayers on a housing project. Each was allowed to choose his team mates to form eighteen four-man work teams. Twenty workers were given

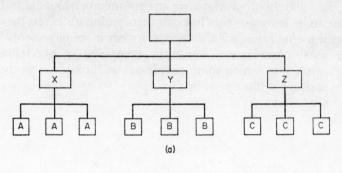

(a)

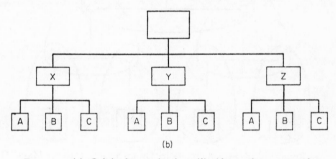

(b)

FIG. 23.—(a) Original organization. (b) Alternative suggested.

their first choice, twenty-eight had their second choices, sixteen obtained their third choices and the eight isolates were distributed over the groups. As a result labour turnover decreased from 3·11 leavers per month to 0·27 and labour costs were decreased.[88]

One major difficulty, however, in using sociometric methods for team selection is that teams of unequal ability and capacity may result.

The Link-pin Theory

If problem-sharing between superiors and supervisors and between supervisors and employees is an effective way of integrating work group goals and organization goals, then each supervisor and superior should belong to two different levels of work group; the work group composed of his subordinates and a work group which includes his own boss. Such considerations lead Likert to suggest that management should build up work groups and link them in the overall organization by means of people who hold overlapping group membership. This has come to be known as the 'link-pin theory' though Likert prefers to call it the 'interaction influence system of management.'[89] His ideal organization would be composed of overlapping work groups in which some people act as 'link-pin' members. The position is illustrated in Fig. 24.

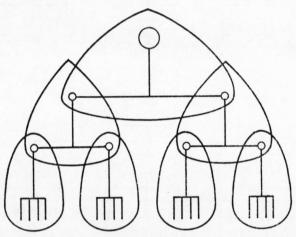

FIG. 24.—Rensis Likert's overlapping Work Group Structure. (After Mason Haire (ed.), *Modern Organization Theory*, p. 193, John Wiley, London & New York.)

The superior in the bottom group is a subordinate in the next group and so on through the organization. Specialists would also be integrated into these work groups and the groups used for decision-making and not simply for communication. Likert does not use the term 'committee' since committees do not necessarily allow the full participation which would be essential to effective functioning.

Likert's link-pin theory has been critized even by fellow-psychologists. Robert Dubin, a sociologist at Oregon, condemns the overlapping group form of organization on the ground that it is often wasteful and slow.

'At the level of linking organization units, the analogical application of the group-dynamics precept leads to a preference for circular linkage-systems. This takes the typical form of permanent committees made up of unit representatives, *ad hoc* committees, periodic meetings of representatives of "interested" units, or the persistent demand that everybody be "kept informed" of developments in each unit. The volume of activities involved in this togetherness, as well as the gamesmanship employed to carry it through, is what has given rise to Parkinson's Law, and parallel, but less exact formulations of it.'[90]

A more serious criticism of Likert's theory is that it presupposes that co-operation is the sole factor that is needed to optimise a business situation. Group participation, in any case, is not always best. Even Likert emphasizes that people should not participate beyond their expectations. Many decisions, too, made by managers do not affect directly any work group, for example those on company insurance. An excellent guide to deciding the appropriateness of group decision-making is the following set of criteria established by Robert Tannenbaum and Fred Massarik.

'1. *Time Availability*. The final decision must not be of a too urgent nature. If it is necessary to arrive at some sort of emergency decision rapidly, it is obvious that even though participation in the decision-making process may have a beneficial effect in some areas, slowness of decision may result in thwarting other goals of the enterprise or even may threaten the existence of the enterprise. Military decisions frequently are of this type.

2. *Rational Economics*. The cost of participation in the decision-making process must not be so high that it will outweigh any positive values directly brought about by it. If it should require outlays which could be used more fruitfully in alternative activities (for example, buying more productive though expensive equipment), then investment in it would be ill-advised.

3. *Intra-Plant Strategy*

(*a*) *Subordinate Security*. Giving the subordinates an opportunity to participate in the decision-making process must not bring with it any awareness on their part of unavoidable catastropic events. For example, a subordinate who is made aware in the participation process that he will lose his job *regardless* of any decisions towards which he might contribute may experience a drop in motivation. Furthermore, to make it possible for the subordinate to be willing to participate, he must be given the feeling that no matter what he says or thinks his status or role in the plant setting will not be affected adversely. This point has been made effectively in the available literature.

(b) *Manager Subordinate Stability.* Giving subordinates an opportunity to participate in the decision-making process must not threaten seriously to undermine the formal authority of the managers of the enterprise. For example, in some cases managers may have good reasons to assume that participation may lead non-managers to doubt the competence of the formal leadership, or that serious crises would result were it to develop that the subordinates were right while the final managerial decision turned out to be in disagreement with them and incorrect.

4. *Inter-Plant Strategy.* Providing opportunities for participation must not open channels of communication to competing enterprises. "Leaks" of information to a competitor from subordinates who have participated in a given decision-making process must be avoided if participation is to be applicable.

5. *Provision for Communication Channels.* For participation to be effective, channels must be provided through which the employee may take part in the decision-making process. These channels must be available continuously and their use must be convenient and practical.

6. *Education for Participation.* For participation to be effective, efforts must be made to educate subordinates regarding its function and purpose in the over-all functioning of the enterprise.'[91]

There is a reluctance to concede that the more powerful the work group becomes, the more the pressure to conform increases on any 'odd man out' and, in the process, both his happiness and freedom are reduced. Participation is also difficult to structure in practice, and this difficulty partly arises because there is doubt about the motives which participation is meant to satisfy. The following are possible.

(i) It satisfies some need for affiliation or some desire to associate with one's colleagues.

(ii) It satisfies the desire to feel of some consequence by giving people a say in their own destiny. Participation brings about a more uniform distribution of power in an organization, and as a consequence, autocratic behaviour is more difficult.

(iii) Participation by eliminating extreme viewpoints through social pressure brings about a reconciliation of viewpoints.

(iv) It leads managers to consider the perceptions of the man on the shop floor and so take them into consideration when planning changes. For example, technological changes may be resented, not because progress itself is resented, but because such change can alter existing social relationships.

Determining which of the above is most important will decide the approach to achieving participation. Until deeper analysis is forthcoming, it is best to regard participation as involving all the above aspects.

DELEGATING AUTHORITY

Definition of Authority

In the classical approach, authority was defined as the institutionalized right to make decisions and to give orders to subordinates on behalf of the company. Many have felt that such a definition does not reveal the fundamental features of authority in that, in a final analysis, the amount of authority possessed by someone is measured by the extent to which he can guide the behaviour of others without their questioning his direction. Thus H. A. Simon, borrowing heavily from Chester Barnard, states that a subordinate accepts authority whenever he permits his behaviour to be guided by others without independently examining the merits of the decision.[92] Authority on this view is the ability to make decisions that are unquestioningly obeyed. It thus stems from the recipient of orders and not the order-giver or the organization itself. It is the recipient of orders who decides which orders to accept, though his 'area of acceptance' is dependent on the perceived consequences of his refusing any particular order. This, in turn, is affected by the sanctions— limited today—available to the order-giver. Every manager has a sense of how far he can 'push' his subordinates, and this limit may have little reference to the nominal rights given to his position.

Many people are irritated by arguments over definition as they appear to be merely arguments about words. Such a view is erroneous. The arguments, for example, whether law is to be regarded as a principle certified by reason, or a command, or an agreement, are not just academic debates. When one definition is accepted rather than another, then one set of attributes of the subject is accepted as being more fundamental than another set. The consequences deduced from a definition depends on which set of attributes is stressed. If we accept Simon's definition of authority, the following consequences can be deduced.

1. Simon himself points out that authority in his sense need not be exercised only in a downward direction, though it is in practice mainly exercised in this manner. When a superior accepts a recommendation from a subordinate without re-examination of its merits, he is accepting the subordinate's authority.

There are, however, further consequences.

2. The allocation of authority as indicated in position schedules does not depict the actual pattern of authority, but rather the authority that is expected to prevail in the normal course of events. Hence, it follows that the delegation of nominal rights to give orders may not mean the delegation of real authority unless the delegation is also accepted by those on whom the authority is to be exercised. Management can deceive itself, by allocating nominal rights, into believing that they have given the subordinates the means to do the job. In allocating authority, the emphasis should not be on what authority it is desirable for an executive to possess, but on what authority it is practically possible to delegate.

Wilfred Brown of Glacier Metal recognizes the limitations to formal authority and, as a consequence, has set up a formal legislative system composed of the various power groups to gain approval of what he considers to be beyond his authority.

'When such changes are felt by the Chief Executive to exceed the bounds of the authority which has already been invested in his role, he must seek an extension of that authority. In order to do this, he brings into play certain social mechanisms, e.g. meetings of Boards of Directors or meetings of shareholders, testing of customers' reactions through a sales organization, meetings with representatives of employees. In so doing, he is precipitating interaction of the Executive System with these power groups and interaction between the power groups. This interaction is legislative by nature.'[93]

3. A superior should try to influence rather than seek to exercise authority. When one person is influenced by another, there is no unquestioning obedience but a change in behaviour as a result of being persuaded. As a consequence, influencing people to change is more effective than ordering people, since orders run the risk of not being obeyed, which in turn weakens the existing authority relationship.

4. In Simon's definition, authority is exercised over people. On this basis it would be incorrect to speak (say) of the authority to dispose of certain resources where only one person is directly involved. Legal rights would be exercised rather than authority in the same way that a person exercises his legal right in disposing of his own house.

The Simon analysis of authority does focus attention on aspects of authority which are important and, in certain situations, fundamental. His authority defines *actual* authority whereas the classical approach defined *formal* authority though Fayol did point out that the right to command did not necessarily imply the capacity to command.

Work Group Authority

If the overlapping group form of organization is the organization of the future, then the work group may be the ultimate source of power in the future. Mason Haire states:

'It seems to me that the tendency to internalize the ultimate seat of authority will go on in the corporation and that it will shift farther and farther inside. I suggest that it will be shifted from being grounded in the professional manager, and the process of management, until it is ultimately grounded in the work group itself. The final source of authority will be the authority of the work group. The final control will be self-control; the self-control will come from the individual's commitment to the organization, and the individual's commitment will come from his integration into the general goals and activities of the organization.'[94]

H

In Fig. 25, Mason Haire traces the stages through which power has and will change hands with the passage of time. It raises two problems. Are the stages inevitable as Haire suggests?

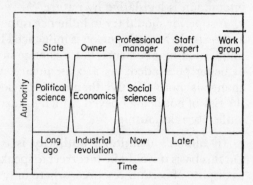

FIG. 25.—The rise and fall of power in industrial organizations. (Diagram by Mason Haire in G. B. Strother (ed.), *Social Science Approaches to Business Behaviour* p. 165, Tavistock Publications, London, and Richard D. Irwin, Homewood, Ill.)

Haire is not suggesting that all work groups within an organization—on a one-group, one-vote arrangement—will have equal power any more than different managers have equal power in an organization at present. He is, however, suggesting the inevitability of management by work group. Although Fig. 25 is plausible, we should not confuse a logical order with an inevitable evolutionary order; stones arranged in an ascending order of magnitude may form a logical order but not an evolutionary one. Although participation is likely to increase (and there is scope for some increase) there is no reason for believing that work groups are the best means of making decisions in all spheres. As long as there are situations where work groups are inefficient, and as long as many people believe that decision-making by work groups is equivalent to 'the supremacy of ignorance over knowledge and numbers over instruction', the spread of management by work group will be restricted. Many, too, may agree with Brown that 'if a manager is over-easily persuaded by his subordinates, he will find himself carrying responsibility for decisions that his own judgment had, in fact, rejected.'[95]

SPECIFYING RESPONSIBILITY

The classical approach claimed that each person in the organization should know his responsibilities so that accountability for performance is clearly established.

A criticism of this approach is that too much emphasis on

staff assessment and defining responsibilities promotes competition when co-operation may be more desirable. Inter-personal competition should be stimulated only where men's work is independent rather than interdependent, and where there exist objective assessments of performance. Otherwise, inter-personal competition leads to frustration and conflict, and overall efficiency is sacrificed. The more complex the business, the more interdependence increases so that performance on a job depends on how well a number of people have co-operated. In such circumstances, it is pointless to judge a person as if he were independent. On these grounds many recommend a loosely structured organization where emphasis is on teamwork rather than on individual responsibility, though it is hoped that group pressure eliminates any tendency to slack. Few, however, would perhaps go as far as Mason Haire does in the latter part of the following statement where some kind of motivated anarchy is recommended:

'The next big thing that would have to be changed would probably be the neat job descriptions. Such descriptions are typically set up to tell a man exactly what he should do and exactly where his bailiwick ends. They are designed to eliminate conflict in the system. An alternative approach to the organization might well be to permit overlapping and conflict in areas of responsibility, hoping to encourage the initiative and to utilize the conflict rather than to smother it.'[96]

The viewpoint expressed in the previous section should not be automatically accepted. As Wilfred Brown points out, a manager who 'does not know what decisions he can or cannot make . . . in doubt he is likely to follow a course of doing nothing at all. . . . I have found, however, particularly in discussing jobs with external applicants, that the array of policy represented by our Policy Document, Standing Orders and Directives, causes people to assume the precise opposite of the real situation, i.e. that this extant written policy will deprive them of the right to make decisions. In fact, it is only by delineating the area of "freedom" in this way that a subordinate knows when he can take decisions. The absence of written policy leaves him in a position where any decision he takes, however apparently trivial, may infringe an unstated policy and produce a reprimand.'[97]

Interdependence of work does not necessarily exclude a fair
assessment of each person's contribution; the individual foot-
baller's performance depends to some extent on the play of his
colleagues, but few would dispute that individual assessment is
possible. It is the nature and degree of interdependence that is
all important. The whole problem was one of which Henri
Fayol was very much aware: 'it is increasingly difficult to
isolate the share of the initial act of authority in the ultimate
result and to establish the degree of responsibility of the
manager.'[98]

It could be argued, in fact, that as organizations become
more complex there is an increasing need for individual
assessment since it becomes even more difficult for each
employee to assess his own strengths and weaknesses, and his
contribution to overall goals. Knowledge of progress or knowledge of results is important psychologically for two reasons.
Without knowledge of results, no learning occurs. One famous
psychologist is reputed to have said that the old adage that
'practice makes perfect' should be changed to 'practice makes
perfect providing there is knowledge of progress.' How can
people improve if they are not aware of what they are doing
wrong? A second reason for providing knowledge of results is
that even when people are competent at a job, knowledge of
results helps performance. A number of experiments have been
made which indicate that knowledge of results acts as an
incentive to effort, particularly if such results are used by a
manager to encourage rather than reprove the employee. Of
course, where there is interdependence there is a tendency to
blame others for personal failure, but the frequency and
magnitude of the resulting conflict can be exaggerated. This
may seem to outweigh the advantage of keeping people on
their toes by providing each individual with knowledge of his
performance. In any case, even when teamwork is emphasized,
serious conflicts can still arise through disputes about people
pulling their weight.

Other criticisms have been made of individual performance
assessment.

1. A too-heavy emphasis on individual evaluation leads
management to neglect the development of well-knit work
groups. Communication is also distorted. The supervisor (to

use the language of Roethlisberger) becomes the master of 'double talk' or the master of 'translating what is into semblance of the way it ought to be.' The supervisor is under pressure to misrepresent events so that there is no reflection on his ability. As a consequence, facts are distorted and superiors are kept in ignorance as to the true state of affairs. The supervisor is also tempted to channel his attention upwards rather than to the needs of the people under him, and to neglect those lateral or cross-relationships which become more important as the firm grows in size.

2. Too much faith can be placed on setting standards. Performance is often measured by a standard on one factor when several factors would have to be taken into account if overall performance was to be measured. In the absence of any such multi-factor standard, it is not known whether the increased effort on one standard leads to decreased effort elsewhere. Even if a multi-factor standard does exist there is the problem of weighting the factors according to their relative importance.

3. Brown, while stressing the importance of assessing individual performance, points out that many facets of performance cannot be quantified.

'(a) How much change in method ought a subordinate to have developed in the way he does his job, as a means of improving it, over a given period of time?

(b) Should he have been able to foresee trouble that did, in fact, arise: and should he have been ready with a solution?

(c) Is it his fault that some of his own subordinates are of poor calibre and have not performed well; or does this trouble arise because of the policy operated by the Company with regard, say, to salaries, which has led to a situation where he has been unable to get together as good a team as necessary to do the job at the required standard?'[99]

Although it is agreed that 'double talk' and the distortion of true goals are dangers that are inherent in situations where there is an emphasis on individual accountability, it is also true that these dangers need never manifest themselves as they result not from personal evaluation but from the way the evaluation programme is administered.

Plans are not self-realizing, but need to be communicated to those responsible for their execution. Standards define these plans since standards represent satisfactory performance on objectives. Without standards—explicit or implied—there is no real planning nor can any guidance be given. Standards are essential even though management's efforts at setting them may be both imperfect and approximate. However, it is no use setting standards unless action is to be taken on deviations, and this inevitably involves taking action through people. This necessitates appraisal of subordinates. A major error in setting standards lies in setting them on the wrong factors—on factors that are easy to measure rather than on factors that are indicative of performance. There is, of course, the problem of weighting for the relative importance of factors if one overall multi-factor standard is to be set. However, even where weighting is difficult so that performances on each factor cannot be amalgamated into one index, the several indices of performance can still be revealing since performance can be low on all factors.

Many who do not criticize the setting of standards criticize the way they are set and communicated to employees. Many favour the work group setting its own standard as in the Harwood case. The superior discusses with his subordinates the need for some common yardstick for judging performance. If there is agreement on the need, subordinates are then asked to list the major segments of their job. Standards to reflect performance on the major job segments would be set by the group itself whether the group was a shop floor group or a management group. Although standards set in this way may be only a slight improvement on the historical position, it is maintained that these will be gradually raised if subordinates continue to review and set their own standards with the superior in the background encouraging them to greater efforts. Where there are difficulties in assessing performance on an individual basis, then the group would set standards for itself as a whole. However, even with individual assessment, the corresponding standards would be set collectively. In this way, group pressure is used to reinforce individual commitment and standards can be adjusted for ability so that each person enjoys some success experience.

Where such participative methods are possible, there is much to recommend the above approach. A compromise solution is that used by the author on a number of occasions with office staff. Each clerk would set his or her own target each week, but management would also indicate the performance they believed could be attained by the competent worker during the hours actually spent on the job. Each clerk is merely encouraged to improve on his historical performance, but the more objectively set standard gives management a guide as to individual strengths and weaknesses, and also avoids the situation where poor performers became prematurely self-satisfied.

ESTABLISHING RELATIONSHIPS

The relationships which are of interest are social ones. Of particular importance are the concepts of 'status' and 'role'. 'Status' refers to the position a person occupies within some system of social relationships, such as a work group or society, while 'role' refers to the pattern of behaviour attributed to, and expected from, that status. Different statuses are of differing importance and desirability while roles are differentiated by the corresponding tasks. Status and role are of significance since they influence a person's behaviour towards other people and so influence behaviour within an organization.

Within the work group, group norms influence a group member's behaviour. However, behaviour is even more precisely determined by the status and role a person occupies in a group. Behaviour is, in addition, influenced by status and role in *past* groups and by expectations about likely status in other groups. Because of these reference groups, people having identical roles may behave differently or people occupying different roles may behave alike. The ambitious young man employed as a foreman may not behave towards his subordinates, his peers and superiors in the way other foremen do because he has high expectations about future promotion. Similarly, the fact that a shop steward wishes to rise within the trade union movement will affect his behaviour with colleagues and in negotiations with management.

Each person occupies several roles since he belongs to a number of groups and he has different patterns of behaviour to go with each role. He behaves differently in his roles of worker, father, club member, church member and so on. People are expected to change roles as they move from one position to another; the managing director is not expected to behave at a company party as he does at work.

Within the organization, the division of labour and the authority structure create different roles though the informal organization within the work group gives each person an additional role and status.

The concepts of status and role are important because:

1. The creation of positions with conflicting roles should be avoided if possible. Roles inevitably on occasions do conflict. The foreman who sees his friend and subordinate violating some strict company rule is in a role-conflict situation. However, a person should not normally be given responsibilities which conflict. The sales manager should not be asked to reduce stocks of finished goods and at the same time provide a better service to customers.

2. People gauge the status of others not by careful analysis but by status symbols. The size of the person's office, the rug on the floor, the job title, and so on, are generally taken as indicators of status. Such symbols can be conferred as an organization incentive or to achieve personal responsibility. On the other hand, once conferred, they are difficult to remove and organization changes should take account of them if resistance to change is to be minimized since a loss of status is a 'loss of face.'

3. Too much emphasis on status within an organization may inhibit communication and reduce co-operation.

4. Organizations can be regarded as a fabric of role relationships. However, the activities and expectations officially laid down for some role may be essentially different from what happens in practice. Thus a contrast can again be made between the formal organization and the informal. People of similar official status may rank differently in informal status or prestige and it is the informal status that influences behaviour. In general, some attempt should be made to reconcile the informal and the formal if conflicts are to be avoided and plans successfully implemented.

WORK ORGANIZATION

The work necessary to achieve company objectives has to be broken down and parcelled out among those within the organization. The classical approach emphasizes the economies that result from task specialization. The human relations school points out that specialization can be carried too far so that an employee carries out 'merely a motion rather than an integrated job,' and work fails to stimulate high performance. Thus Argyris of Yale speaks of excessive task specialization as follows: 'It inhibits self-actualization and provides expression for a few, shallow, skin surface abilities that do not provide the endless challenge desired by the healthy personality.'[100] Argyris maintains that under conditions of high-task specialization, the employee's attitude is likely to be apathetic and indifferent towards management and its goals. Furthermore, he predicts that such apathy and indifference will result in demands for increased wages, 'not as rewards for production but as management's moral obligation for placing the employees in the kind of working world where frustration, failure and conflict are continuously being experienced.' In other words, the worker will view any wage demand as a compensation for frustration.

What does the human relations school suggest is an answer to high task specialization? Some argue that the only real solution is 'job enlargement', enlarging the job so that it utilizes more than the superficial skills of the employee. The answer cannot lie in more selective recruitment since, even if selection procedures were advanced enough to separate those to whom high task specialization would be acceptable, too few such people exist. Similarly, job rotation is viewed as a mere palliative. There are a number of cases where it is claimed job enlargement has led to increases both in the quality and quantity of output. One well-described case is that quoted by Drucker about the job enlargement carried out at IBM in America:

'But each job is designed so as always to contain a challenge to judgment, and an opportunity to influence the speed and rhythm of a man's work.

'The story goes that Mr Thomas J. Watson, the company's president, once saw a women operator sitting idly at her machine. Asked why she did not work, the woman replied: "I have to wait for the set-up man to change the tool setting for a new run." "Couldn't you do it yourself?" Mr Watson asked. "Of course," said the woman, "but I am not supposed to." Watson thereupon found out that each worker spent several hours each week waiting for the set-up man. It would, however, only take a few additional days of training for the worker to learn how to set up his own machine. Thus machine set-up was added to the worker's job. And shortly thereafter inspection of the finished part was included, too; again it was found that little additional training equipped the worker to do the inspecting.

'Enlarging the job in this way produced such unexpected improvements in output and quality of production that IBM decided systematically to make jobs big. The operations themselves are engineered to be as simple as possible. But each worker is trained to be able to do as many of these operations as possible. At least one of the tasks the worker is to perform—machine setting, for instance—is always designed so as to require some skill or some judgment, and the range of different operations permits variations in the rhythm with which he works. It gives the worker a real chance to influence the course of events.

'This approach has not only resulted in a constant increase in productivity at IBM, but has also significantly affected the attitudes of workers. In fact, many observers both inside and outside the company think that the increase in the worker's pride in the job he is doing is the most important gain.

'The policy of "maximizing jobs" has also enabled IBM to create significant opportunities for semi-skilled workers. In each foreman's department now there are one or more "job instructors". These are senior workers who do their own work but who also help the other, less experienced workers learn higher technical skills and solve problems requiring experience or judgment.'[101]

Many psychologists condemn production layouts that are designed to isolate one individual from another. Such an attempt to cut down on wasteful gossip may lose more through increased labour turnover and absenteeism. A changeover to a production layout that allows people to mix freely with each other may decrease absenteeism and improve performance; other ways should be found to discourage idle gossip.

Trist views a production system as being made up of both a technological organization (equipment and lay-out) and a work organization relating the people to the job. Technological, psychological and economic factors can conflict. Optimization of the overall system must give due weight to each of these factors; seeking to optimize on just one factor leads to sub-optimization. Minute specialization may confuse task and role relationships and inhibit the development of well-integrated work groups. The formal organization should not inhibit the development of the informal organization which can be used to strengthen it.

A number of comments on job enlargement and job satisfaction can be made.

(i) Many cases quoted on job enlargement do not give sufficient details of the existing specialization to justify the conclusion that subsequent increases in production result from job enlargement. The existing specialization may have entailed poor team balancing so that combining activities may bring about an increase in output.

(ii) Job enlargement is likely to be most effective in conditions such as assembly line work where each individual is currently performing only one operation in the assembly. In such circumstances, specializing on any individual job may frustrate though carrying out the whole assembly may be both challenging and satisfying. However, these circumstances do not always operate. Enlarging one man's job may mean making another man's less interesting. Menial work is given to juniors not only to economize on scarcer skills but also to relieve more senior people from chores. Forming work groups with interchangeable tasks may cause resentment among those of higher status if they are called on to perform low-status work.

(iii) There is no guarantee that if jobs are enlarged so that they represent a challenge to the worker, performance will automatically increase. Neither job enlargement nor job satisfaction in general can guarantee an increase in output. Job enlargement, like other incentives, is hardly likely in itself to provide a sufficient condition for ensuring high performance. On the assumption that management is purely concerned with efficiency, it must weigh up the technical gains arising from minute task specialization against likely losses resulting from the employee being dissatisfied with his job. The difficulty lies in assessing this balance. The essential point of job enlargement is to provide jobs that represent a challenge; *doing* the job must be satisfying, not just *having* the job. At present there appears no objective criterion and management must rely on judgment and consultation in deciding the degree to which it is profitable to carry out job enlargement.

FINAL COMMENT

The human scientists have much to offer. Some, however, write more like evangelists than scientists and with an aggressive dogmatism that is more a reflection of faith than evidence. These people do more to annoy than to convert and make many businessmen dismiss (with slight basis in fact) all the findings of social psychology, on the ground that such findings are merely a collection of warped perceptions based on poor experimentation and inadequate sampling. Perhaps we shall always have to tolerate the extremists so that we can find out something from the others.

CHAPTER IV

THE SYSTEMS APPROACH

SYSTEMS DEFINITION

A system is a set of interdependent parts which together form a unitary whole that performs some function. Essentially, the parts must be interdependent and/or interacting. A heap of components may form a 'whole' but not necessarily a system unless arranged, say, to form a machine. Any system can be shown to be a sub-system of some larger system. Thus a carburettor is a sub-system of the car engine and a sub-sub-system of the car itself.

In order to understand how a system fulfils its function, it is useful to know how all its parts are related to each other and how the system is to be linked to the larger system that constitutes its environment. The way a watch measures time can be deduced by knowing how its parts are related to each other and the way it conveys time can be deduced by studying how it is used—that is, by studying the watch/user relationship.

This discussion raises two important questions. How are the boundaries of any system determined? What are its appropriate sub-systems? The answer to both questions depends on the purpose of the analysis, and incorrect answers can lead to errors. Take, for example, the design of a machine such as a lathe. It is common to treat the machine itself as the system. In consequence, inadequate attention is given to the physical limitations of the human operator. Ergonomists today speak of the 'man-machine' system to emphasize that the system often consists of both man and machine, and consequently machine parts such as levers and dials need to be designed with human physiology in mind. In another sphere, those engaged in analysing clerical procedures emphasize that each procedure must be looked at as a whole so that the needs of all users are adequately considered. An order-handling procedure is interdepartmental and must be designed to serve the needs of all the departments concerned

with order handling—production, sales, accounting and so on
—it should never be designed purely with one department in
mind.

Many national controversies are in part arguments over the
appropriateness of the system. Is it possible to make a study of
national transport needs by a study of railway economics in
isolation? Can one study the training of physicists and chemists
by studying merely their education at university level and
ignoring schools? Even where people are agreed about the
purpose of an analysis, there may still be debate over system.
The difficulty or cost of dealing with the complexity of a larger
system may make for the acceptance of something less than
ideal. A case can usually be made out for studying some larger
system. Thus Susan Stebbing, a logician, commented on
physics:

'In order that physics as a science should be possible, it is
necessary that we should be able to consider some characteristics
in isolation from other characteristics. It is in fact the case that
physicists have been successful in regarding the physical world
as separable into small systems, and into sub-systems of those
systems, with respect to which physical statements can be made.
It may be true that

> Thou canst not stir a flower
> Without troubling of a star,

but it must be admitted that no one stirring a flower has ever
succeeded in observing the consequent troubling of a star.
Astronomers have prosecuted their researches in the confident
belief that in turning their telescopes upon the moon they have
in no way affected that which they are observing.'[103]

This debate over system is not merely academic. To study
too wide a system for the purpose at hand is wasteful, but to
study too narrow a system may lead to sectional efficiency at
the expense of the total system. If a particular system seeks to
achieve certain objectives at minimum cost, it is not likely to
do so by seeking separately to minimize cost for each of the
sub-systems, since overall minimum cost may necessitate high
cost in one sub-system to achieve low cost elsewhere. For
instance, a motor manufacturer might reduce the cost of piston
rings by increasing their production and consequently spreading

the fixed costs: but unless he can simultaneously make more pistons and cylinder blocks he will only increase the overall cost by accumulating an expensive surplus. It is the interdependence of sub-systems from the point of view of the purpose at hand that necessitates the overall approach.

The purpose of an analysis also determines which sub-systems are appropriate. If we wish to understand how a watch works, it is of little value to study how the gold parts are arranged in relation to the brass parts if they are purely ornamental. In studying a watch as a mechanism, aesthetic aspects are irrelevant. However, in any study of the watch as a marketable commodity, the system would include the watch's appearance as one important sub-system.

THE SYSTEMS APPROACH TO ORGANIZATION

The systems approach emphasizes that for any investigation there is an appropriate system to be studied, and the purpose of the investigation decides both the boundaries of the system and the appropriate sub-systems. If the investigation concerns company organization, what is the system to be studied? The organization of the company is a means to achieving its objectives. Thus the system must embrace both the company itself and that part of the external environment, for example the market, that impinges on objectives, so that these can be set as a basis for organization. What are the appropriate sub-systems to be studied? The sub-systems chosen centre on the main decisions to be made to accomplish objectives. The organization should be designed to facilitate decision-making, but since decisions depend on information and information on communication, the organization is built up from an analysis of information needs and communication networks. Decision-making is chosen rather than activities or departments because it is through the process of decision-making that objectives and policies are laid down and actions taken that result in company success or failure.

The systems approach to organization consists of the following steps.

1. Specifying objectives.

2. Listing the sub-systems, or main decision areas.

3. Analysing the decision areas and establishing information needs.

4. Designing the communication channels for the information flow.

5. Grouping decision areas to minimise the communications burden.

SPECIFYING OBJECTIVES

Devising a system that pursues the wrong objectives solves the wrong problem. This may be far more wasteful than choosing a system that fulfils objectives inefficiently. A company that sets an objective purely in terms of volume sales may devise the ideal marketing campaign to achieve this objective but may go bankrupt while doing so. The problems involved in specifying objectives have already been discussed. Despite the difficulties encountered, setting company objectives is essential if guide lines are to be provided for decision-making throughout the company.

LISTING THE SUB-SYSTEMS, OR MAIN DECISION AREAS

In listing the decisions that are to be made within a company, a difficulty arises in that all problems cannot be anticipated, so that appropriate decisions cannot always be predicted. Another difficulty lies in determining the unit of decision since almost every decision is part of a system of decisions. As Simon illustrates:

'The minute decisions that govern specific actions are inevitably instances of the application of broader decisions relative to purpose and to method. The walker contracts his leg muscles in order to take a step; he takes a step in order to proceed toward his destination; he is going to the destination, a mail box, in order to mail a letter; he is sending a letter in order to transmit certain information to another person, and so forth.'[104]

The unit of decision is a matter of judgment depending on the purpose and therefore the detail of the analysis. The problem is illustrated in the case study (Appendix I).

ANALYSING THE DECISION AREAS AND
ESTABLISHING INFORMATION NEEDS

Decision-making means making a choice from a range of possible courses of action. Managers aim to be efficient at making decisions, that is, choosing the alternative which, as far as they can tell, will give better results as measured by their objectives than the alternatives displaced.

It is not immediately apparent that decision-making is any problem. Superficially, it appears to be merely a matter of getting the facts on the grounds that when these have been examined the right solution or decision will automatically present itself. Decision-making is usually more complex than this. Many important decisions have to be made without knowledge of all the facts and are often more akin to acts of faith. Decision-making deserves detailed study since the success of a company depends on the quality of its decisions.

Effective decision-making depends on how well the following steps are carried out.

Establishment of Goals

Like the company itself, every decision seeks to further some goal or objective. A decision on inventory level might seek to choose the level which minimizes the costs of carrying inventory plus the costs of running out. Decision goals, like company objectives, can be multiple and conflicting. However, since all goals are meant to further company objectives, conflicts need to be resolved by choosing those goals that will best further these objectives. In practice, it may be difficult to show explicitly the relevance to company objectives of decisions made lower down in the organization, such as decisions on leave of absence.

The choice of a wrong decision goal means that the wrong problem is put forward for solution. A sales manager may be simply given the goal of increasing turnover by 10 per cent. If literally pursued, the attainment of the goal might lead to unprofitable sales, which may not have been the intention of those who laid down the goal. An interesting example of the importance of defining the right goal or problem to be solved was mentioned by Mountbatten in an interview recorded in *The Observer* Colour Supplement, September 6th, 1964, in referring to the work of Sir Solly Zuckerman:

'Solly had been asked to work on the general problem of how much bombing was required to "silence a battery". Being a scientist, and a man with a very logical and original mind, he asked a question which nobody seemed to have asked before:

I

"What does 'silence' mean? Does it mean drop a bomb on every gun, and put it out of action, does it mean knock out the men firing the guns, or what?" His point of view was, you can't answer the question "What is required to silence a battery?" unless you can define what you mean by "silence".

'What Solly found, in a nutshell, was that if you knocked out one-third of the guns only, by that time the noise and the blast, the disruption of communications, and the general alarm and excursion had such an effect on the morale of all the troops in the vicinity that you had virtually silenced the whole battery. On this basis, Pantelleria was far from being impregnable. He was right. We took it with a loss of only three men.'

Identifying possible Courses of Action

The essence of decision-making is that the manager has to make up his mind which course of action to choose. However, the posing of different courses of action for consideration is not straightforward. Simon points out that they are not usually given but must be sought, so it is necessary to include the search for alternatives as an important part of the process of decision-making. The words 'searching for alternatives' seem a little misleading as this suggests that the decision-maker already knows what he is looking for. This may not be true. Hence it may be better to speak of the 'process for identifying possible courses of action.'

Since the process for identifying possible courses of action determines what is considered, it is also a factor in determining the quality of the decision finally taken. A manager may simply adopt what others have done in like circumstances and not worry about identifying possible courses of action. The danger is that standard solutions are installed when conditions are far from standard and goals are distorted to suit the solution. The processes for identifying possible courses of action range from 'brainstorming' to sophisticated management techniques such as those of Operational Research. Management techniques are becoming more and more important in identifying alternatives. For example, one company wished to increase its sales of men's socks. The different courses of action suggested by reflection were to have a 'sock sales week' and/or increase expenditure on advertising socks. A market analysis, however, showed that the company only catered for about 15 per cent of the men's sock market and might profitably consider producing 'fancy socks' and socks at another price level.

Identifying Consequences

Every course of action will have a set of consequences if chosen. Again, the consequences attached to alternatives are seldom given but have to be identified. Often only major consequences are listed and side-effects ignored. In particular, the side-effects on morale of decisions made within a company have tended to be ignored.

Knight, the economist, has suggested a classification of the conditions under which decisions are made.[105] Decisions can be made under conditions of certainty, risk and uncertainty. A decision under certainty occurs if each possible course of action has a unique outcome. In these conditions, choosing among outcomes or consequences is the same as choosing among the possible courses of action. If the courses of action can also be ranked in order of preference, decision-making is made routine. A decision under conditions of risk means that more than one possible outcome or set of consequences is associated with each course of action, but that probabilities for the outcomes can be stated. Finally, decision under conditions of uncertainty means that more than one possible outcome is associated with at least one of the different courses of action but that probabilities for the outcomes cannot be stated. It is doubtful whether managers ever feel that they make decisions in conditions of complete uncertainty. In fact, specialist advice might increase the manager's uncertainty when making a decision by showing the decision to be more complex than previously envisaged. Shackle, another economist, speculates that in conditions of uncertainty the manager 'feels' out his experience and chooses a course of action that causes him to feel some degree of certainty that no unpleasant surprise will occur.

The management sciences have developed an operational language for expressing risks and techniques for measuring it. Of particular importance is the application, since World War II, of mathematical and statistical techniques to management problems, aided when necessary by electronic computation. However, Simon argues that 'many, perhaps most, of the problems that have to be handled at middle and high levels in management have not been made amenable to mathematical treatment, and probably never will.' Simon also considers how to improve the problem-solving capabilities of humans in 'non-programmed' situations and how computers might be used to aid managers in problem solving without first reducing the problems to mathematical or numerical form.[106] Ashby's work on the mechanization of thought processes is also relevant to this problem.[107]

All the management sciences seek to provide information to reduce uncertainty. If a new product is launched without any market analysis, the decision is made under conditions of uncertainty. The information resulting from a market analysis and pilot venture could reduce uncertainty and transform the decision into the category of risk.

The more decision-making can be simplified, the more it can be formalized, in which case the decision may either be delegated or sufficiently programmed to be passed on to a computer. Decision-making is also simplified by formulating policy, since information on policy removes a great deal of uncertainty within the organization. Policy can be regarded as a set of rules for reaching a decision. Where such rules can be developed, consistency in decision-making throughout the organization is more likely and time is saved because less reference is made to superiors.

Managers seek to reduce uncertainty in decision-making. Galbraith, the economist, even argues that 'the development of the modern business enterprise can be understood only as a comprehensive effort to reduce risk.'[108] He criticizes theoretical economists who assume managerial behaviour to be explained simply in terms of a need to maximise profit. Managers may in fact sacrifice additional profit in favour of certainty. The results of an investigation by Meyer and Kuh[109] would tend to support Galbraith. They found that businessmen favoured the internal financing of capital investment and tended to limit this investment to the amounts that were available within the company. They tended to ignore the market rate of interest and business opportunities that could only be financed by external borrowing. It is argued that this behaviour occurs because the consequences are far more serious if an externally financed investment fails than if the investment is internally financed. However, an equally plausible explanation is that people carry over into business life their personal dislike of borrowing.

Establishing Criteria for Evaluating Consequences

The decision goal determines the criterion for evaluating the various sets of consequences. There is a need, however, for measuring the extent to which an event furthers objectives. A common unit of measurement is necessary to resolve conflicts. Without it, one cannot compare, say, the alternative that leads to lowest distribution costs and the alternative that achieves shortest delivery time. Unfortunately, all consequences cannot be expressed precisely in terms of their effect on cost and profit so there may be difficulty in using money as the common unit of measurement. This may lead to a complex problem of value measurement which has been the concern of Von Neumann and Morgenstern.[110]

Establishing Decision Rules

If consequences are evaluated by predictions of their effect on profit, it would be consistent to choose the alternative that is likely to add most to profit. The answer may not be so easy. There is the problem of the conflict which might arise between long- and short-term profit expectations. There is also the difficulty of relating profit to risk and uncertainty. A low profit with low risk may be more acceptable than a high profit with high risk. Profit expectations alone may not tell the whole story. Certain of the alternatives may have consequences which are not susceptible to measurement but none the less can be very important. The manager may choose not the 'best' alternative as judged on quantitative grounds but some other alternative that he considers is more likely to further his goals.

Example

The decision process as described above can be illustrated by a simple example. A company wishes to increase its profits by introducing a new product. Alternative products are considered. The managing director asks for likely sales on the two products. Sales department claims that 150,000 units of Product No. 1 can be sold but only about 100,000 units of Product No. 2. However, questioning reveals that the forecasts are not certain but contain an element of risk and sales forecasting produce ranges of possible sales and attached to each range the probability of actual sales falling within that range. The costing

department calculated net profit on the assumption that the
mean of each range was likely to be the actual level of sales if
sales fell within that range. The managing director then

	Anticipated Sales	Probability (a)	Net Additional Profit (b)	Profit Expectation (a × b)
			£	£
Product	30,000	0·2	4,000	800
No. 1	90,000	0·25	8,000	2,000
	150,000	0·3	12,000	3,600
	210,000	0·25	16,000	4,000
			Total	10,400
Product	20,000	0·1	3,000	300
No. 2	60,000	0·1	8,000	800
	100,000	0·5	10,000	5,000
	140,000	0·3	15,000	4,500
			Total	10,600

FIG. 26.

decided that of the two products he would select that which
was likely to yield most profit overall. Fig. 26 gives all the basic
data. Profit expectation is found by multiplying the probability
figure by the net additional profit figure and the total profit
expectation is simply the sum of the products. On the basis of
the data in Fig. 26 the managing director would choose
Product No. 2 which gives the highest profit expectation.
However, the difference in profit expectation between the two
products is so slight that other non-measurable considerations
might lead to Product No. 1 being chosen instead of Product
No. 2.

A final comment on decision-making lies in Simon's argument that no manager explores all alternatives but terminates
his search when a satisfactory rather than a best solution has
been discovered. ('Always be content with the third-best
solution. The second-best comes too late and the best never
comes at all'—A. J. Rowe.) The manager's behaviour is
'satisficing' rather than maximizing. Alternatives are separately
sought and evaluated and the search to identify further alter-

natives is only continued if no alternative is found to be satis-factory. The cost and difficulty of identifying alternatives and the urgency of the solution will have a bearing on what is considered satisfactory.

Information Needs

The discussion on the decision process itself is important. It shows how decisions can be simplified, which is important when determining the level to which decisions can be delegated. Furthermore, the discussion has shown that the quality of decision-making depends on the quality of the information available as well as on managerial judgment. Information to management has been said to provide the same function as headlights to the night driver. The headlights illuminate the road ahead but do not rule out the need for good judgment. The informational system does affect organizational planning. It ought to influence the level at which delegation takes place. Also, since information needs to be communicated, it deter-mines the communication network, which, in turn, is facilitated or hampered by the organization structure. Finally, informa-tional requirements may necessitate the setting up of specialist departments whose job it is to provide the appropriate informa-tion to management. Such specialist departments need to be integrated into the company and so affect any organization plan.

A planned management information system has as its goal an integrated system of reports that gives each level the 'right' information at the 'right' time so that decisions are based on the best information available, as far as the provision of such information can be justified on economic grounds. There are a number of different approaches to an information system. One approach is to design quicker ways to process data. This approach is useful in situations where information needs are well established and speed has some merit, for example in accounting, records for legal purposes, or an air-raid warning system, but is not very helpful in situations where information needs are only vaguely known. Another approach is to increase the amount of data available. This approach can often lead to the collection of useless information. Another approach is to examine existing reports for duplication and so avoid the situation where sales and production (say) are producing the same statistics. This approach may merely reduce the cost of doing the unnecessary. Finally, managers may order certain reports to be discontinued and only re-introduce them when individuals protest. This approach may lead those who have been deprived into producing their own unofficial records and reports. The most fundamental approach is the 'decision approach' which consists of specifying the decisions to be made and then determining information requirements. This is the more logical approach since the purpose of information is to facilitate decision-making. All information systems must be tailor-made to suit specific circumstances and each report forming part of a management information system should satisfy criteria as to relevance and adequacy, cost in relation to usefulness, timeliness, accuracy and precision, and presentation. *Relevance and Adequacy.* All decision-making is concerned with formulating plans or controlling the execution of plans. Hence, information is needed for either planning or control. Planning looks ahead to determine what is to be done while control currently establishes whether plans are being or are likely to be achieved.

If an existing or proposed piece of information or report is to be useful in planning it must facilitate one or more of the steps taken in making a decision by

(i)   providing information on goals,
(ii) identifying the alternatives or ruling out a whole class of alternatives formerly thought possible,
(iii) showing the consequences likely to arise from adopting an alternative,
(iv) helping to evaluate alternatives.

If an existing or proposed information system is to be adequate for planning purposes, it must be concerned with the major uncertainties—that is, concerned with the uncertainties in the main decision areas as deduced from objectives, past company history and forecasts.

When plans are formulated, expectations are laid down about the conditions which must exist if the plans are to be satisfactorily carried out. Each expectation is termed a 'standard' and the difference between actual achievement and standard is calculated as a basis for control. Thus, let actual achievement $= A$ and standard $= S$, then $A - S = D$, the difference. If D is outside acceptable limits, either actual performance is above or below what might reasonably be expected, or expectations were set too high or too low in the first place. Control is being exercised wherever this comparison is made between what is happening and what was intended if the purpose is to reduce the error between the two. Thus if S refers to the anticipated cost of a product or a process, it is termed standard cost and D is the variance. If S refers to the anticipated cost of a department or the company as a whole it is referred to as a budget and the formula $D = A - S$ represents the process of budgetary control. There are many other control systems and all possess an underlying unity of concept which is not always recognized. The systems analyst in describing this unity uses a number of terms which may be unfamiliar, many being taken from control engineering.

The measurement and comparison of actual with standard and subsequent corrective action is referred to as 'feedback'. Technically, feedback means transferring a portion of the energy from the output of some device back to its input to achieve control. It can be regarded as checking on the output of some process and controlling the input to the process in accordance with the effectiveness of the output as judged against standard. Such an arrangement in which the input depends on feedback from the output is known as a 'closed-loop control system'. If the feedback reduces the error, that is the difference between actual and standard, rather than aggravates it, the feedback is termed *negative*. Positive feedback aggravates the error.

Fig. 27 is a model of a closed-loop system with negative feedback; the model is more descriptive than that represented by $D = A - S$. It could represent a machine with a built-in control mechanism such as a thermostat regulating the temperature of a house. The input is the labour and fuel needed to keep the furnace going. The processor is the furnace itself and the output is the heat entering the room. The thermostat would include some mechanism to detect the actual room temperature. If the thermostat dial were set at 70°, this would be the desired output or standard. Where the actual temperature varies from 70° some controller switches the furnace on or off. The system would be closed-loop or closed-cycle because the input of labour and fuel depends on the actual output of heat. If the input were modified as a result of directly sensing the actual disturbing influences outside the house, the system would be 'open-loop'. Open-loop systems may be more effective in certain business

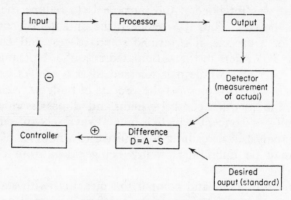

FIG. 27.—A closed-loop system with negative feedback.

situations since, unlike error-regulated systems, they can achieve perfect control in theory.

The model in Fig. 27 is general and could even represent overall company control. Inputs would be labour, orders, materials, capital and information. Outputs would be products and services to customers and dividends to shareholders. Company objectives would express the desired outputs. Control would seek to nullify the random effects of fluctuating orders, material supplies and to detect and pursue trends as a basis for revising objectives.

Controls serve a number of specific purposes.

(a) They foster delegation. A reluctance to delegate may be traced to a fear of losing control, reinforced by the knowledge that delegation does not mean being absolved from blame in the event of failure. Budgeting in particular, of all management control systems, has been instrumental in fostering delegation and facilitating decentralization. As the economist Neil Chamberlain comments:

'The neoclassical school of economists believed that the one sure curb on the expansion of any company was a marginal cost curve which was bound to rise, sooner or later, due to the inability of all factors to increase proportionately; and that the factor which, of all factors, was most certain to be the limiting one was management. More labour and more capital might be added in equal doses, preserving their proportionality, but management—particularly the top-level entrepreneurial type of management—by its very nature had to remain fixed, or relatively fixed, thereby eventually leading to diminishing returns: the job of overseeing the expanding firm would require management to spread itself thinner and thinner, becoming less and less effective, until rising costs would put an end to its growth. The process of budgeting, with its potentialities for decentralization, no longer makes this expectation so certain. At a minimum, it increases very considerably the size to which a firm may grow before diminishing returns set in. The weight of detail under which it was believed that top management's effectiveness would be smothered has been distributed to others farther down the organization; the necessity for close supervision has been lightened through the concepts of budgetary responsibility and management by exception.'[111]

(b) They save managerial time. Controls save managerial time by focusing attention purely on significant deviation from plans.

(c) They provide feedback for planning. Past performance helps shape future aspirations and those who do not learn from the past tend merely to repeat their errors. This point emphasizes the fact that the same information may be used for both planning and control purposes.

(d) They measure performance. Because controls measure performance they are often resented. However, such accountability for performance is the factor that facilitates delegation. As management has already found in budgeting, if such resentment is to be avoided without abandoning accountability, then those being controlled should be encouraged to participate in setting standards.

In examining the usefulness of information for control purposes we need to determine whether:

A. The information is complete. Is each of the quantities in the equation $D = A - S$ available? It is frequently the case that standards have not been laid down either implicitly or explicitly during planning and information is merely available on A, the actual state, and management is left to control on this basis.

Without standards there can be no control though standards may be implicit—they may exist but may not be available for reference.

B. The standard has been set correctly. Standards may be based on 'forgotten guesswork'. Any standard should fulfil the following conditions.

(i) It should be reasonably attainable, since a standard represents the conditions that exist if a job is carried out satisfactorily. Standards set too high either cause anxiety or tend to be treated with contempt. Standards set too low tend to breed premature satisfaction and complacency.

(ii) It should be based on certain conditions for its attainment. If these conditions change, so should the standard. Where alternative conditions may be operative then alternative standards may be developed. This is the reasoning behind flexible budgeting; an appropriate expense budget, for example, is developed for each range of possible output levels.

(iii) It should correspond to responsibility. Someone must be made accountable for variation from standard if control is to be effective.

(iv) It should be limited to key activities. Often controls are based on factors that are easy to measure, rather than key. For example, time cards may be the only information that an office manager receives (apart from the limited amount received through visual observation) as to the efficiency of the clerks under him. In such circumstances, it is not surprising that the clerks feel that good time-keeping is mainly what is demanded of them. We cannot possibly control all factors in a situation; control over minor factors dissipates energy.

(v) It should be based on best analysis available. Ideally, standards are based on analysis and measurement and so generate the need for measurement (for example merit rating). However, descriptive standards can in certain circumstances be effective, for instance standards of military dress, and past performance (which may be the only guide, as in the field of labour relations). The setting of standards for any particular activity improves with experience but initially management may have to make do with crude approximations.

(vi) **It should be based on results rather than method.** It is better to set standards on results rather than method; the way the job is done being left to the man himself. In this way self-control is likely to be encouraged and periodic accountability is substituted for close supervision. However, control over results may be too remote or even be impossible, so that control over method becomes essential. In the field of advertising, control must be on method, for example media selection, because the end-results of advertising cannot usually be measured, in the short period, in terms of resulting sales. In such circumstances the standard constitutes a criterion and represents the conditions that exist when the job *is being carried out* satisfactorily.

C. The control information is structured. The various levels in an organization should not receive identical control information since this may bring with it a tendency for superiors to duplicate the work of subordinates. Villiers argues that control reports for the various levels of management should be comparable but related in the same way as an atlas is related to an ordnance survey map.[112] Only the controls reaching the executive with responsibility for taking action should give details of variation from standard. For the executive charged with taking immediate action, the difference or error, D, needs to be broken down and analysed into its constituents but executives at higher levels simply wish to be informed of the variation. If the higher executive wants the details, these are readily available. As an example, a managing director may simply know that costs have risen in factory 'A'. The manager of factory 'A' may know that costs have risen because department 'X' has made excessive scrap during the period under review. Only the foreman in the department knows the various reasons for this excessive scrap as it is his immediate responsibility to take remedial or corrective action. If all levels were to receive the details, they may be overburdened and neglect work that is more pertinent to their immediate responsibilities, or they may be inclined to suggest remedies before the subordinates are given an opportunity to take action. Of course, if unacceptable variations persist between standard and actual, it becomes the responsibility of higher levels to take action.

The PERT/Cost system used for controlling weapon development in the USA provides a perfect example of structured control information.[113]

Cost in Relation to Usefulness. A report or any other piece of information cannot be justified simply on the ground that it is useful for planning or control purposes. Its cost must not exceed the likely benefits derived from its use. The total expenditure on information that is justified on economic grounds will vary from company to company and will also depend on the availability of management techniques for reducing uncertainty. A large firm can usually justify a greater expenditure on providing information than a small firm in the same line of business. A company with a thirty million pound turnover is more likely to justify a ten thousand pound annual expenditure on marketing surveys than a company that only has half a million turnover. However, two companies of such a difference in size might justifiably spend the same amount on information if the smaller company was in a line of business where uncertainty was high while the larger company had a monopoly in selling a standard product to an assured market.

The efficiency with which uncertainty can be reduced depends, among other things, on the development of management techniques. As techniques are discovered and prove their worth, more is spent on securing the services of specialists who use their techniques to produce improved planning and control information.

Information should not be distributed randomly to all and sundry. Cheap duplication of information and the enormous output capacity of the modern electronic computer have tended to encourage the widening of distribution lists while the cost of sorting, filing and reading information has tended to be ignored. Although too little information may lead to wrong decisions, too much information is wasteful of resources and often means that relevant items of information are overlooked in an information jungle.

Timeliness. Information should normally be provided when the best use can be made of it. Although speed should not be sought for its own sake, information consistently late may be useless or lead to action that is inappropriate to a new situation that has developed meanwhile. In the example of the foreman and his scrap, reports on scrap levels which reach him too late cause scrap to accumulate before remedial measures are taken. On the other hand, there is no point in producing information faster than it can be used unless originating it earlier reduces its cost.

Accuracy. Accuracy should not be sought for its own sake. There is often a conflict between providing figures that are accurate to the nearest penny and providing data on time and in a way that is operationally useful. Time is often wasted in computational work by taking figures to an unnecessary degree of accuracy. For sales statistics it may be possible to ignore shillings and pence when the resultant error is insignificant for the purpose.

Presentation. Some engineer once said that the impact of a report depended not only on the weight of its contents but also on the speed with which its message is put across. Good presentation should aim at bringing the significant facts into focus in a language familiar to the reader. A detailed discussion of presentation is outside the scope of this book but there are a number of good books on the subject.[114]

DESIGNING THE COMMUNICATION CHANNELS
FOR THE INFORMATION FLOW

Communication is the means by which information is passed from one person to another and can be carried out by gesture, talk, instrument or written word. It is through communication that information is passed to the decision-maker and resulting decisions passed to those involved in executing them. Without communication there could be no organization since it would be impossible to get people to act in a co-ordinated way; people would be linked together by an abstract chain of command but acting without a chain of understanding. Where communication is poor, co-ordination is poor since co-ordination implies that people are being informed about each other's plans. Furthermore, co-operation presupposes co-ordination so that co-operation itself depends on communication.

An elementary communication system is shown overleaf.

The information source is the origin of the message. The transmitter converts the message into signals and transmits the signals to a receiver over a communication channel. The receiver converts the signals back into a message which is passed over to its destination. The words 'transmitter' and 'receiver' are here used in a general way, and include such

instruments as typewriters, tape recorders, telephones and even
the shorthand notes taken down by a typist. The noise source
adds an interfering signal to the message signals. Noise can be

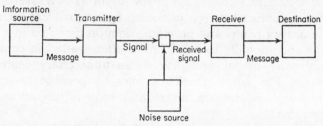

FIG. 28.—(Diagram, Shannon and Weaver.[115])

defined as any addition to the signal which is not intended by
the information source, such as distortions of sound or error in
transmission. The word 'noise' is used in a technical sense. It
may coincide with common usage in a telephone or radio
message, but also embraces a stenographer's errors in shorthand
and typing, misprints by a teleprinter, or even misinterpreta-
tions of a spoken sentence. In oral speech the *information source*
is the brain, the *transmitter* is the voice mechanism, the *communication channel* is the air, the *receiver* is the ear of the listener
and the *destination* is the brain of the listener.

Noise is other sounds that make the message difficult to hear.
Redundancy occurs when there is more information in the
message than is strictly necessary, for example when each word
of a message is repeated. Some redundancy is usually desirable
to correct any errors that might occur in the transmission of a
message. The redundancy in the English language aids the
listener to identify from the context words that otherwise might
be misunderstood. For example, the sentence 'Gd sv the Qn'
would be correctly interpreted as 'God save the Queen'.

Weaver distinguishes three problem areas in communication.

'Relative to the broad subject of communication, there seems
to be problems at three levels. Thus it seems reasonable to ask,
serially:

Level 'A'. How accurately can the symbols of communication
be transmitted? (The technical problem.)

Level 'B'. How precisely do the transmitted symbols convey the
desired meaning? (The semantic problem.)

Level 'C'. How effectively does the received meaning affect conduct in the desired way? (The effectiveness problem.)'[116]

Weaver also states that:

'The mathematical theory of the engineering aspects of communication, as developed chiefly by Claude Shannon at the Bell Telephone Laboratories, admittedly applies in the first instance only to problem A, namely the technical problem of accuracy of transference of various types of signals from sender to receiver.'[117]

He goes on to note, however, that 'the theory of Level "A" is, at least to a significant degree, also a theory of levels "B" and "C"'.[118]

Problem level 'A' is not so important as yet in organization work as to justify full discussion though Shannon's information theory has been applied in work organization.[119, 120] The problem levels 'B' and 'C' are more relevant but the theory is very much in its infancy.[121] Hence this section will confine itself to a general discussion on communication channels.

The line of communication between two people or two organizational units is the communication channel. Thus A —— B indicates that communication exists between units A and B. As this connection does not show whether the communication is one way or two way, it is common to add arrow-heads to indicate the direction of communication. Thus A ←——→ B would indicate that the communication is two way while A ——→ B would mean that communication is merely from A to B. Where several units are linked together by several channels, a communication network is established. A communication network relates people to each other and top management to every unit in the business. An analogy can be found with the human nervous system. The brain cells are linked up with every organ and every tissue of the body through the nerves. Each nerve (or channel) has its special work to do. Some carry messages to the brain, and others, messages from the brain to the cells. The brain receives and examines the information and sends off answers, although much routine decision-making has already been delegated to other parts of the nervous system such as the ganglia. It is interesting to note that any muscle that is cut off from all communication with the brain quickly dies unless the connection is restored.

K

Drawings a-c in Fig. 29 show various communication networks for a group of five people. The question arises as to which network is best. Laboratory experiments undertaken by psychologists Bavelas and Leavitt[122] suggest that the 'wheel' is faster if the problem to be solved is straight-forward, but that the

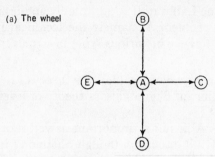

(a) The wheel

'A' in best position to co-ordinate group. Communication position gives him natural leadership advantage

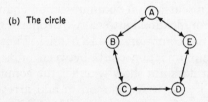

(b) The circle

No participant holds a dominant position

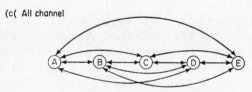

(c(All channel

No participant holds a dominant position

FIG. 29.—Communication networks.

'all-channel' network stimulates high morale and adaptability and encourages accuracy. Likert, with his overlapping work group form of organization, is recommending the all-channel network since this would represent the work group in conference. Committees are generally all-channel unless the chairman insists on all communication being routed through him.

'A', in the wheel, is in the best position to co-ordinate the group. The group are dependent on him regardless of the formal authority he possesses. He may impede or speed up group activity and, since he acts as a filter, he can also influence the attitudes of members to each other. Too many channels may mean that 'A' is overloaded. The wheel may be inappropriate where the group is required to solve a problem that depends on cross-fertilization of ideas. Suppose the marketing director below has to decide market strategy

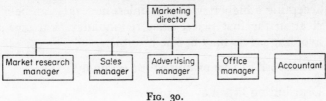

FIG. 30.

What communication network should be adopted? The all-channel would be the most appropriate, since the participants will all have ideas of their own which need to be discussed by the group as a whole so that ideas are ventilated and conflicts resolved. On the other hand, if the marketing director merely has to decide the date of the annual sales conference, the wheel would be more appropriate since the director may simply require information from his colleagues as to convenient dates.

A network can be examined in much the same way as information reaching the manager can be examined.

(i) A network may be inadequate. Someone may be missed out of the network who should not be; salesmen may not be informed about a proposed advertising campaign, though such information may be necessary to planning their sales appeals.

(ii) The channel itself may be overloaded; taking the telephone service as an example, this may necessitate

(a) increasing the number of channels;
(b) queueing; on this point Rowe comments as follows:

> The flow of information can introduce time lags into a system as a result of queueing effects. In a sense, information flowing through a number of decision makers is comparable to jobs flowing in a factory or cars flowing on the

highways. For example, if the decision-maker is viewed as a processing centre, the rate of arrival of decisions and the time taken to make the decision will determine the average delay or queueing effect. If appropriate priorities are assigned the various decisions to be made, it is possible to both improve effectiveness and reduce delay times. Another means of reducing delays is to have alternate channels for the given decisions. Filtering or screening decisions is still another means of reducing the flow time through the system[123];

(c)   accepting a higher error rate unless messages can be made clear in the first place, since redundancy as a means of avoiding errors may not be possible.

(iii) A network can be examined for economy.

(a)   Distribution lists may be too wide.
(b)   The information source and destination could perhaps be located nearer to each other.
(c)   The channel itself may not be the most efficient available.

(iv) A network may also be too slow. Transmission times may be calculated for each channel and the total time compared with that desirable as a basis for considering other networks. Forrester of the Massachusetts Institute of Technology has shown how internal delays in communication can produce oscillations in outputs and stock levels which may be wrongly attributed to environmental factors.[124]

GROUPING DECISION AREAS TO MINIMIZE COMMUNICATIONS BURDEN

As specialization increases, interdependence increases and with it the need for co-ordination. How much interdependence can be tolerated without giving rise to a serious failure in co-ordination, assuming that the people concerned are willing to co-operate? The answer depends on:

1. *Channel capacity.* The information capacity of a channel is the maximum rate of transmitting information that is possible through the channel. The greater the channel capacity relative to communication needs, the greater the tolerance for interdependence.

2. *Stability of interdependence.* The more stable the work relationships between organization units, the greater the tolerance for interdependence since stability facilitates prediction, so co-ordination may be achieved by a plan and this reduces the need for subsequent communication. In an example given earlier, it was argued that sales training could be carried out by the personnel department because co-ordination by plan was possible. The syllabus, etc., could be agreed, say, each year between sales and personnel staff and there would be no need for them to keep in constant touch with each other. Where relationships are in a state of flux, co-ordination must be achieved by constant feedback since the unpredictability of events rules out planning in advance.

The systems approach lays stress on minimizing the communications burden to improve co-ordination. Grouping people under a common superior and putting them physically close to each other may reduce the communications burden and, therefore, may be one way to improve co-ordination. Looking at the company as a whole, if co-ordination is the goal, then groupings should be chosen which lead to more self-containment than alternative groupings; information sources, decision and action points most dependent on each other are grouped together. The pattern of interdependence between units may also be made more stable by grouping units under a common superior so that co-ordination is improved by having all units subscribe to a common plan.

Some writers aim at a broad systems approach without the detailed analysis of decisions and information flows as described above. For example, Rice speaks of his **Import—Conversion —Export** model, derived from open systems theory which he describes as follows:

'When a complex enterprise is differentiated into parts, the sub-systems that carry out the dominant import-conversion-export process, that is *perform the primary task of the enterprise, are the operating systems.* Generally, there are three kinds of operating systems:

(*a*) import—the acquisition of raw materials;
(*b*) conversion—the transformation of imports into exports;
(*c*) export—the disposal of the results of import and conversion.

In simple organizations there may be incomplete differentiation and one operating system may carry out more than one part of the total process, or even all of it; in complex organizations there may be more than one operating system of each kind. Most organizations will contain a mixture of both simple and complex structures.'[125]

Further descriptions of his model might be summarized as follows:

Where there are several products, there may be several major operating systems (subdivision on the basis of major differences in sources of raw material), several conversion systems (subdivision on the basis of differences in technology or process sequence), and several export systems (subdivisions on the basis of the differences in distribution). Each operating system, too, can be further subdivided into smaller discrete systems in that each has its own primary task and hence its own dominant import-conversion-export process (in other words each is a system in its own right and so could be further subdivided on the basis of its having an input which is processed, and an output which results from the processing). Since a system external to the operating systems is required to control and service them, there is also a need for a managing system which contains management plus the control and service functions (such as finance, personnel, and research and development). Rice refers to his initial division of an enterprise into operating systems and a managing system as the first order of differentiation. Where the operating systems and the managing systems are further subdivided, the result is second-order of differentiation; further subdivision leads to third-order of differentiation, and so on. Control and service functions come under the management within whose area the functions exclusively operate.

The main criticism of this approach by Rice is that it is at too high a level of generality to be useful in detailed organization planning. In fact, it differs little from the approach put forward by some 'classical' writers who argued that the first step in company organization was to define the operational departments which were, generally, Purchasing (Import), Processing (Conversion) and Distribution (Export), and then to distinguish the specialist departments who help management to co-ordinate and control these operational departments. Furthermore, they argued that grouping within these divisions could also then be carried out on the basis of grouping together those activities that came nearest to serving common goals.

THE SYSTEMS CONTRIBUTION TO CLASSICAL ORGANIZATION PROBLEMS

GROUPING INTO DEPARTMENTS AND HIGHER ADMINISTRATIVE UNITS

The systems approach is mainly concerned with grouping to achieve co-ordination. The approach recommends listing the main decision areas within a company and determining the information needed for the decision to be made effectively. Activities may then be grouped to minimize the time spent in communicating this information. Co-ordination is thus facilitated by having the 'right' information communicated to decision-makers with minimum delay arising as a result of the organization structure.

The time spent communicating information is not usually the sole criterion used by systems analysts in considering the problem of grouping. The decisions that give rise to the communications are considered.

1. It may be undesirable to group together specialist staff, such as quality control experts, and decision-makers whose functions are directly affected by their recommendations, as this may result in limiting the activities of the specialist staff as well as affecting their objectivity.

2. Speed in communicating information is more vital in some decision areas than in others. In the event of conflict between alternative groupings, speed must be taken into consideration.

Most companies are organized on a functional basis; each department is devoted to some function—production, marketing, and so on. This type of departmentalism is not appropriate in all circumstances and some firms have moved over to what is termed 'project management'. This can be regarded as divisionalization on the basis of project. The firms adopting some sort of project management—the British Aircraft Corporation is one of them—generally fall into the following categories.

(i)   They are engaged in designing and building large plant or machinery to customer specification.

(ii) They depend on product innovation since the products they produce are quickly obsolescent.

(iii) The product or project is technically complex and requires a great amount of development work by a number of different technical specialists.

(iv) The product or project must be produced to a rigid time schedule to meet customer specification or market demand.

Firms falling into one or more of the above categories are likely to find a major problem in co-ordinating activities on a project. In these circumstances, a company organized into functional departments may find its organization is slow, cumbersome and inflexible. The specialists concerned with some project need to be brought together, not scattered widely throughout the departments. They also need to give their undivided attention to one project so that their contribution can be relied on. They may also need to be placed under a common superior responsible for the overall direction of the project.

The situation may be looked at from a systems viewpoint. The need for co-ordination on a project may be far greater than the need for co-ordination between projects. Alternatively, co-ordination between projects can be planned well in advance whereas co-ordination on a project requires day-to-day consultation among those concerned with it. The information required for the successful completion may be much less concerned with what is happening on other projects than with what is happening on the project itself. Communication networks, if drawn, would be distinguished on a project basis. Project management thus leads to grouping those decision areas most dependent on each other.

The need for project management has often been indicated by the use of network analysis[126] but has sometimes led in the first instance to the matrix type of organization as shown in Fig. 31. In this form of organization, the specialists concerned with the project report both to a functional boss and to a project co-ordinator. The specialist is both a member of a functional group and also of a project team.

The matrix organization does not always lead to the degree of project control considered necessary, and conflicts may arise between the functional manager and project co-ordinator. As a consequence, firms may move on to project management

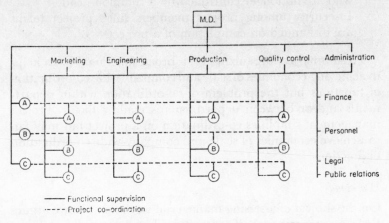

FIG. 31.—'Matrix' organization.

where the specialists are allocated to a project for the duration of its life and are answerable only to the project co-ordinator until the project is finished. The aim has been to make the project team as self-contained as possible. This may result in duplication and under-utilization of resources, but such waste may be a reasonable price to pay for achieving co-ordination.

Companies do not go to the extreme in project management but retain some functional departments as some overall company direction is necessary. Furthermore, to split all departments on a project basis (the legal department is a good example) may be manifestly less efficient than retaining some departments to serve the company as a whole.

Project management has been effective in achieving co-ordination on a project; in developing strong teamwork and teams which identify themselves with project goals. However, there still remains the problem of setting these advantages against the following losses.

(i) Under-utilization of resources in order to achieve self-containment of projects.

(ii) Failure to achieve some economies of scale.

(iii) Failure to achieve co-ordination of functions company wide. There is a difficulty in maintaining standards of proficiency and uniformity of practice among specialists who are no longer controlled by a common head.

(iv) Insecurity among project members since project teams are disbanded on completion of a project.

To summarize, organizing on a broad functional basis helps in achieving economies of scale and company wide co-ordination of functions but the problem of co-ordination within departments and/or between departments is made difficult. Project management simplifies co-ordination on a project but may fail to achieve economies of scale and company-wide co-ordination of functions.

Workload

On the subject of assessing managerial work load, Rowe argues that an economic span of control could be determined as shown in Fig. 32.

FIG. 32.—Distribution of economic span of control. (From A. J. Rowe, 'Management Decision Making and the Computer', *Management International*, 2/1962, by permission of Betriebswirtschaftlicher Verlag.)

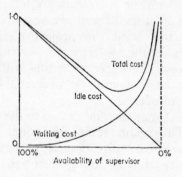

'Since the supervisor is a decision processor, an economic span of control could be determined as shown in Fig. 32. If the supervisor is always available (no subordinates), there would be a high idle cost; however, if there were too many subordinates, decisions would be held up due to the supervisor being unavailable. This leads to a high waiting cost. Thus, the correct span of control would consider the cost of delays in decisions on the entire business. Since the waiting or queueing effect increases exponentially, it appears that there is an optimum availability of the supervisor which can be related to the span of control.'[127]

Rowe is rightly pointing out the queueing aspects of the work load problem since it may not pay to cater for peak work load conditions. However, his exposition is inadequate as it ignores, like the classical approach, the fact that a manager carries out work other than that arising through having subordinates.

DELEGATING AUTHORITY

Communication can be from the information source to the decision-maker or from the decision-maker to the point of action. If the information source and the point of action are fixed, then the communications burden can only be reduced by varying the point of decision. In these circumstances, the delegation of decision-making authority assumes major importance in organization. Also, unless it is known who makes what decisions it is not possible to determine the distribution of information.

Network Centrality

Communication networks provide an insight into the problem of allocating decision-making authority. As Simon states:

'The possibility of permitting a particular individual to make a particular decision will often hinge on whether there can be transmitted to him the information he will need to make a wise decision, and whether he, in turn, will be able to transmit his decision to other members of the organization whose behaviour it is supposed to influence. . . . An apparently simple way to allocate the function of decision-making would be to assign to each member of the organization those decisions for which he posesses the relevant information. The basic difficulty in this is that not all the information relevant to a particular decision is possessed by a single individual.[128]

As an extension of these ideas in simple problem solving, decision-making tends to gravitate to the person at the centre of the communication network.

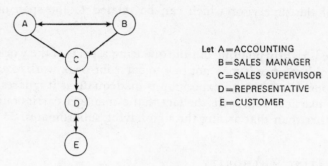

Let A = ACCOUNTING
B = SALES MANAGER
C = SALES SUPERVISOR
D = REPRESENTATIVE
E = CUSTOMER

FIG. 33.

Suppose, for example, the above network is appropriate for making a decision about closing an account on economic grounds. All the executives in the network have some information to contribute which is relevant to the decision, but who should actually make the decision? In this simple instance, a good case can be made out for allowing the decision to be made by the person in the centre of the network; calculated as follows. First, all links or channels through which a person must go to communicate with someone else are added up. Thus, in the case above,

For 'A' AB = 1, AC = 1, AD = 2, AE = 3, making 7 in all.
For 'B' BA = 1, BC = 1, BD = 2, BE = 3, making 7 in all.
For 'C' CA = 1, CB = 1, CD = 1, CE = 2, making 5 in all.
For 'D' DA = 2, DB = 2, DC = 1, DE = 1, making 6 in all.
For 'E' EA = 3, EB = 3, EC = 2, ED = 1, making 9 in all.

The totals add up to a grand total of 34. This grand total is divided by each individual total to find the centrality of each position. On this basis,

A's score is 4·9
B's score is 4·9
C's score is 6·8
D's score is 5·7
E's score is 3·8

In cases where the 'right' decision depends on information being supplied by all participants, and the decision is almost self-evident when all such information is assembled, then the correct decision can be made quickest by the person with the highest centrality score. In the case above it is C, the sales supervisor, so all information should be sent to him to make the decision.

There are many limitations to allocating decision-making authority in this way.

(*a*) All decision-making is not of the problem-solving variety where the decision is a simple inference from facts supplied by all in the network. In the case above, for example, B may bring to bear on the information supplied by others an experience that would not be elicited unless he had looked at all the information together. This is particularly true in cases where the decision to be made is of a qualitative nature.

(*b*) The approach assumes that each participant has the same amount to contribute to the solution of the problem. It may well be that one participant has most of the information with which he is already familiar. Even though this person may not be in the centre of the network, it may still be quicker for him to make the decision since any other person in the network would have to assimilate the bulk of information already held by him.

(*c*) Even where decision-making is in the nature of simple problem-solving, speed in decision-making is not the only factor that should be considered. Cost affects the choice of decision level as well as speed. In certain cases it may pay for a decision to be made at a level lower than that indicated by the centrality position on the ground that the loss in speed is more than compensated by the saving in cost. Ensuring the quality of policy decisions may also outweigh considerations of speed; the repercussions from an error in decision-making, if great, may lead to the decision being made at a higher level than suggested by the centrality position.

(*d*) The network only considers the making of the one decision. Decisions, when made, are conveyed to others to help them make their decisions, but the person in the best position to make a decision may not be in a best position to communicate it to others.

(*e*) The highest centrality score may be obtained by a specialist but it may still be advisable for the specialist to remain purely advisory.

In determining the point at which each decision should be made, the systems approach takes into account the factors mentioned by the other approaches.

The classical approach would consider

1. the cost of decision-making at various levels,
2. the decreased cost or increased effectiveness resulting from economies of scale and/or improved co-ordination.

The human approach would tend to concentrate on decision-making in certain cases by work groups.

However, the systems approach re-emphasizes the fact that co-ordination is improved if communications are improved and decision-making can be speeded up if the decisions are made at the point where the communications burden is minimized. This occurs, in certain cases of simple problem solving, at the position which is the centre in the communications network.

In project management, the project co-ordinators are managing teams of specialists. The problem of who makes what decision is almost always determined by the team members' speciality. There is probably no need for much formality. Similarly, there may be no need to specify how a man should do his job, since he is a professional, though he still needs guidance on objectives. Also, the responsibilities of the project manager and his team are often made clear without formal schedules, since attached to the projects themselves are defined budgets, goals and time schedules. The project team recognizes its responsibility for meeting these targets. The lack of formality is avoided not because formality encourages rigidity, but because authority and responsibility are made clear in other ways.

SPECIFYING RESPONSIBILITY OR
ACCOUNTABILITY FOR PERFORMANCE

Appendix II shows how decision-making authority might be allocated in a way that pays attention to information and communication requirements, and at the same time indicates the subtlety of the decision-making process by recognizing, for example, that many decisions result from team work though the final decision may be taken by one man. This schedule has been successfully used in practice but varies in format to suit particular circumstances. The one shown is designed and completed for the marketing department of 'Strongwear'; a company used as a case study at the end of this section. The first three pages show the allocation of authority over field salesmen and the rest of the schedule shows the allocation of authority for the main marketing decisions. The abbreviations used are explained on the schedule. The column headings are as follows:

(i) *Decision Area.* In this column are entered the decisions to be allocated. The size of decision unit is a matter of judgment depending on the extent to which decision-making is likely to be diffused in an organization. For example, in some companies the three separate decisions listed under 'Work Methods' might be combined into one decision—'determining work standards'.

(ii) *Makes Recommendations.* Into the column 'makes recommendations' is entered the title initials or code number of those who, through having undertaken no specific study of the decision in question, should nevertheless be in a position to make recommendations because of their general experience. They are specifically encouraged, by being included in the schedule, to make suggestions as part of their job.

(iii) *To be Informed After Decision Made.* Into this column is entered the title initials of those to be informed after the decision is made to allow them to carry out their own work.

(iv) *Information Source.* Relevant information improves decision-making but obtaining such information may involve consulting others or reports produced by them. However, the information source limits the range of discretion open to the decision-maker. The decision-making may in fact be purely nominal and routine as when the superior gives such close direction that he lays down not only the decision goal but also how alternative courses of action are to be sought and evaluated. At the other extreme an information source may be purely advisory, as, for example, when the Market Research Manager gives advice to the Marketing Director. Somewhere in between the information source simply gives direction on goals. In this schedule a superior can never be in the position of 'advisory only' to a subordinate decision-maker as advice from a superior is really direction. As Brown points out 'clearly, if a manager gives "advice" to a subordinate, he expects it to be accepted, and he cannot escape the responsibility for having done so. Advice is a confused way of giving an instruction.'[129]

(v) *Makes Decisions*. Although emphasis has been placed on simplifying decisions, there are also cases where circumstances change and make decision-making more complex. As a consequence, although the making of a particular decision may, as a general rule, fall within the province of a particular executive, there are always circumstances where the executive's good sense tells him that he should refer the decision 'upstairs'. Hence, it is realistic to divide the column 'makes decisions' into the two categories shown—those who usually make the decisions and those who only do so in exceptional cases.

(vi) *Appropriate Information*. Into the column 'appropriate information' can be entered the titles or numbers of those documents that are relevant to the decision. Where no information is available, one should ask whether it should be provided.

ESTABLISHING RELATIONSHIPS

The systems approach emphasizes decision-making and communicating appropriate information to the decision-maker. In the process, the way people are linked together for the purpose of making some decision is revealed. Showing the way people contribute to various decisions in this way also makes explicit their formal relationship to each other.

WORK ORGANIZATION

More and more, teams of workers carrying out mainly physical activity are being replaced by machines tended by one or two controllers. The ergonomist specializing in systems work is concerned with the design of these man-machine systems. The emphasis is not on how work should be shared out among workers but on how work should be divided between man and machine. The ideal division changes as technical advances are made; man can still read handwriting better than any machine though this may not always be so.

The division of work between man and computer is of particular current interest. The ideal division in this case does not, however, depend simply on advances in technology but on the extent to which decision-making can be formalized. Where decision-making can be reduced to following a set of rules, it can be made into a routine and handed over to the computer. In such circumstances, though, it may be more logical to regard the decision-maker as the man who makes the rules while the computer may be regrded as merely supplying answers.

As decisions are simplified they can be delegated to lower levels in the organization. On the other hand, it has been argued that the use of a computer may bring with it a tendency to centralization. This is not necessarily so. A computer may provide information that was not previously thought possible and may thus simplify decision-making, allowing it to be pushed downwards. Furthermore, the ICI Mercury computer at Wilton is connected to other divisions all over the country by tele-printer links. This principle is being extended in modern time-sharing computers, which are large machines capable of accepting several quite different jobs and scheduling their performance within the machine.

The more decision-making is simplified, the less the opportunity for exercising judgment. Hence there appears a possibility of conflict between decision simplification and job enlargement. This is to confuse job enlargement with making all work non-routine. Thus Simon comments:

'Implicit in virtually all discussions of routine is the assumption that any increase in the routinization of work decreases work satisfaction and impairs the growth and self-realization of the worker. Not only is this assumption unbuttressed by empirical evidence but casual observation of the world about us suggests that it is false. I mentioned earlier Gresham's Law of Planning—that routine drives out non-programmed activity. A completely unstructured situation, to which one can apply only the most general problem-solving skills, without specific rules or direction, is, if prolonged, painful for most people. Routine is a welcome refuge from the trackless forests of un-familiar problem spaces. The work on curiosity of Berlyne and others suggests that some kind of principle of moderation applies. People (and rats) find the most interest in situations that are neither completely strange nor entirely known—where there is novelty to be explored, but where similarities and programs remembered from past experience help guide the exploration.'[130]

L

POSTSCRIPT AND SUMMARY

This book has attempted to show how all three approaches have something of value to contribute to the overall study of organizations, and how, in many cases, the approaches complement and reinforce each other. As the book moved from a study of the classical, to a study of human relations and systems, there was no suggestion that this was a movement from error to truth. Skill in designing an organization lies in selecting factors drawn from all the approaches that are appropriate to the specific situation under investigation. A summary of the various suggestions follows. Organization design is still very much more of an art than a science with the absence of measurement in the field. The development of suitable methods of measurement is almost certain to be one of the major developments in the future.

SUMMARY

All approaches stress the need to set objectives, so that we do not merely think of better ways to organize the unnecessary or cheaper ways of achieving unsatisfactory end-results.

Classical Problem Area	Approaches to Classical Problem		
	Classical	Human Relations	Systems
1. Grouping into sections and higher administrative units.	Factors considered relevant to grouping: (a) Work load. Keep work load on supervisor or manager to within physical capacities. A company would only need one manager if there was no limit to the work load he could bear. Factors relevant to work load on supervisor: i. Extent to which guidance must be given to subordinates. ii. Extent to which subordinates are trained. iii. Extent to which subordinates are co-operative. iv. Extent to which control information available. v. Extent to which 'policy' laid down so that subordinates can make decisions for themselves. vi. Extent of work other than supervision.	(a) Avoid over-specialization of sections as this leads to sectionalism. (b) Choose supervisors who are employee-centred and who allow subordinates to participate in decision-making. (c) Let team members select each other. (d) Give formal recognition to work group—allow them to participate in decisions that affect them. (e) Use an overlapping work group structure to achieve co-operation. (f) Choose 'flat' as opposed to pyramid structure.	Concerned with grouping to achieve co-ordination. (a) The more opportunity (channel capacity) for communicating, the more interdependence between administrative units can be tolerated. (b) The more the pattern of interdependence between units is stable, then the more the toleration of interdependence since co-ordination can be achieved by long-term planning rather than by feedback. (c) Where speed is paramount, then grouping should be

Classical Problem Area	Approaches to Classical Problem		
	Classical	Human Relations	Systems

	(b) Economies of scale:
	  i. Technical.
	  ii. Managerial.
	  iii. Financial.
	  iv. Marketing.
	  v. Risk Spreading.
	Economies under the above heading may be reaped by grouping like activities together.
	(c) Co-ordination.
	The greater the degree of co-ordination, the more individual efforts are integrated during performance instead of reconciled afterwards. A grouping that minimizes the co-ordination problem achieves the highest degree of self-containment in each administrative unit of the company. Absence of co-ordination leads to:
	  i. Lack of consistency in goals.
	  ii. Wrong timing.
	  iii. Inadequate action.
	  iv. Excess costs in achieving co-ordination.
	Unity of direction principle—activities coming nearest to serving common goals grouped together (principle is vague and ambiguous).
	(d) Nature of activity.
	This can influence the level of grouping, e.g. 'Keyness' of activity, co-ordinating nature of activity.
		i. More authority pushed downwards.
		ii. Superior/subordinate relationship less formal.
			carried out to minimize the communications burden.
			(d) Where co-ordination needs compete, attention paid to:
			  i. Amount of communication between units, i.e. frequency of inter-action for decision-making.
			  ii. Stability of relationship between units.
			  iii. Nature of decisions shared between units.
			  iv. Desirability of speed in decision-making.
			(e) General approach—list main decision areas and determine information needs. Activities grouped to minimise communication.

Above factors (a) to (d) are often in conflict. There is a need to reconcile them. Companies tend to organize their major groupings on a functional basis to achieve co-ordination of functions company-wide and to reap economies of scale, but this makes co-ordination of functions within a department difficult.

2. Delegating authority.

Definition: Formal Authority = institutionalized right to make decisions and give orders. The broad grouping of activities into sections, depts., etc., merely defines lower limit to amount of authority that can be delegated. Some decisions may be taken remote from point of execution:

i. To co-ordinate function company-wide.
ii. To co-ordinate interdepartmental activities.
iii. To reap economies of scale.
iv. Because decision may be key.

Several principles quoted:

i. Delegate authority to position where best information available.
ii. Authority to take action should be delegated as close to point of action as possible.
iii. Define job objectives then deduce what authority should be delegated.

Above principles too crude to act as guide lines. There is a need to consider:

i. Cost of decision-making at various alternative positions.
ii. Decreased cost or increased effectiveness resulting from economies of scale and/or improved co-ordination.

Further principle: Authority should be commensurate with responsibility.

(a) 'Actual' authority depends on extent to which orders unquestioningly obeyed. Actual authority:

i. Stems from recipient of orders and not the order-giver.
ii. Need not only be exercised in a downward direction.
iii. Delegation of nominal rights to give orders may not mean the delegation of real authority. Question is what authority will be accepted by those on whom authority is to be exercised.

(b) Use influence rather than formal authority in dealing with people. Formal authority should be used merely to maintain permissive atmosphere.

(c) Give some authority to work groups.

(a) If the information source and the point of action are fixed, then communications burden can only be reduced by varying the point at which decision-made.

(b) Simplify decision-making to facilitate delegation.

(c) Communications improved and speed in decision-making increased if decisions made at position where communications burden minimized.

Classical Problem Area	Approaches to Classical Problem		
	Classical	Human Relations	Systems
3. Specifying responsibility or accountability for performance.	Definition: Responsibility = obligation to carry out certain activities with accountability for performance. (a) Clear assignment—authority and responsibilities should be formally scheduled. (b) Inherent in authority delegation is obligation to set standards against which to judge performance. Vagueness in assigning responsibility leads to confusion and jurisdictional conflict as it is not possible to hold people responsible for non-performance.	(a) Individual assessment can be overdone. It can make for interpersonal competition at the expense of co-operation. (b) Too heavy an emphasis on individual assessment of performance may lead managers to neglect the development of well-knit work groups. (c) Standards may have to be set on several factors if increased effort on one factor leads to decreased effort on another. If a multi-factor standard does exist, there is the problem of weighting the factors according to their relative importance. (d) The more complex the organization, the more interdependence increases and job performance depends on how well a number of people have co-operated. In such circumstances, it is pointless to judge a person as if he were independent.	In allocating decision-making authority, attention should be paid to information and communication requirements and to the subtlety of the decision-making process—information source may limit discretionary authority: i. May direct aims and means. ii. May direct aims only. iii. May be 'advisory'.

(e) Get work groups committed to overall company goals. They will then set themselves high standards in conjunction with supervision and do their own policing. Group pressure thus used to reinforce individual commitment.

4. Establishing relationships among employees.

In order to achieve co-ordination, people within a company should be formally related to each other so that each knows his position in the team.

Relationships between two people:

(a) *Line relationship*
Below Managing Director, each person should be made accountable to someone. This line relationship:
i. Acts as communication channel from top to bottom and so is prerequisite to co-ordination.
ii. Acts as chain of accountability.
iii. Pinpoints co-ordination responsibility. Note: Unity of command principle and principle of one supreme co-ordinator.

(b) *Functional relationship.*
'A' may not have full authority to act in all matters concerning the unit under him. 'X', though outside the unit managed by 'A', may have some formal authority over A's unit:
i. To facilitate company-wide co-ordination of function.
ii. To facilitate co-ordination of interdepartmental activities.

(a) Lateral relationship should be fostered.
(b) Specialists should preferably be part of a work group that includes operational personnel.
(c) Creation of jobs with widely conflicting roles should be avoided.
(d) Too much emphasis on status may inhibit communication and co-operation.
(e) Gap between formal and informal status should be reduced if conflict to be avoided.

Showing the way people contribute to various decisions make explicit their formal relationship to each other.

Classical Problem Area	Approaches to Classical Problem		
	Classical	Human Relations	Systems

	iii. To reap economies of scale.
	iv. 'X' officially provides 'advice' to 'A'. In all the above cases 'X' has functional relationship to 'A'.
	(c) *Personal assistant*
	A person may be related to his superior by giving him and him alone general help with his managerial work.
	Advantages
	  i. Training ground.
	  ii. Relieve burden on top management.
	Against
	  i. P.A. may abuse his position and undermine authority of others.
	  ii. Many P.A.s may reflect inability to delegate.
	Informal relationships:
	(d) *Lateral relationship*
	People at roughly the same level communicate informally to co-ordinate their individual efforts. Saves time in that communication by-passes common co-ordinator which may be desirable for minor issues.
	Relationships between departments
	Operational Depts.—Those depts. which create and sell the company's products.
	Specialist Depts. Those that provide specialist services.		

5. Work Organization, i.e. grouping tasks to form individual jobs.

(a) Break down work to reap economies of specialization as far as volume of work justifies.

Advantages of specialization:
i. Allows intensive use of scarce talents.
ii. Skill increases from constant practice.
iii. Changeover time reduced.
iv. Allows economic use of machinery with less scheduling, queueing or duplication.
v. Training time reduced.
vi. Encourages mechanization.

Co-ordination losses as increasing specialization increases interdependence:
i. Bottlenecks in work flow.
ii. Communication problem to achieve integrated effort means more supervision.
iii. Work duplication.

(a) 'Job enlargement' recommended. Since monotony can be characteristic of job, each job should be designed so that it is satisfying to do —a challenge.
i. Incentive to effort.
ii. Reduces tendency to frustration, therefore less industrial strife.

(b) Production layouts should not be designed to isolate one individual from another. Other ways should be found to discourage idle gossip. Layouts should encourage development of work groups with high morale.

(a) Simplify decision-making to minimize reference to higher authority.

(b) Design job with worker's physiology and mental limitations in mind. Emphasis not on how work should be shared out among workers but on how work should be divided between man and machine.

STRONGWEAR MANUFACTURING: ILLUSTRATIVE SYSTEMS STUDY

THE study is concerned with the marketing department of a company operating in the clothing field with a current turnover of about ten million pounds and a sales force of 120 selling to 20,000 retail outlets within the British Isles.

This marketing department is composed of the sections shown below:

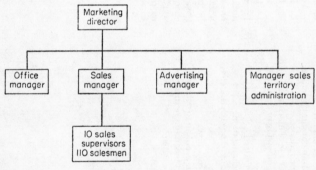

FIG. 34.

The office manager is in charge of order documentation and processing and all customer correspondence. The manager in charge of territory administration produces sales statistics and is concerned with such problems as salesmen's expenses, commissions, territory changes, etc., whereas the sales manager concentrates on controlling selling performance and sales training.

Company Objectives

The aims of the company have never been explicitly stated, but discussion at board level would indicate the following:

Profit. The company is profit oriented and considers a 15 per cent rate of return on total assets to be reasonable. In recent years the profit level has been below this level.

Marketing. The generic need for which the company caters is the need to keep the body covered for comfort, fashion and social reasons. The company caters for several segments of this generic need. In turn, each of these segments can be regarded as generic since the company only caters for some part of each segment. For example, by manufacturing socks and stockings the company caters for the need to cover the foot and lower leg with a soft covering but it only caters for a segment of this need —the adult male's need for a popular-priced, plain sock made from wool or nylon. For the purpose of this broad analysis, a detailed statement on each segment need is omitted. The company aims to sell all its products at current popular prices.

Product Innovation. The company has declared that it intends to produce additional products to satisfy the need for casual, lightweight leisure clothing. It has also declared its intention to abandon production of uneconomic products.

Efficiency. The company is conscious of the fact that its service to customers in recent years has been unsatisfactory. It aims to improve its service by reducing the number of order handling errors and improving the availability of goods, preferably without increasing costs. The company seeks low costs from long production runs by producing a variety of products from the same basic material and design.

Unit Objective

The company aims at achieving a turnover in the next two years of twelve million pounds. The present turnover is ten million pounds. The target turnover has been broken down on a product basis. Market share figures are not currently available. Further investigation reveals that:

(a) a policy of 'blanket' selling is in force. In other words, the company's goods are sold to any outlet that is credit-worthy and can stock the company's goods;

(b) a further policy, when sales costs as a percentage of turnover exceed 5 per cent, is to reduce the size of the sales force and redistribute to the remaining representatives the accounts in vacated territories.

Even without further analysis it is apparent that both these policies are likely to be inconsistent with company objectives. Blanket selling may be poor strategy as it may lead to servicing uneconomic accounts. A fixed, arbitrary ratio of selling costs to turnover is likely to be in conflict with the profit goal as no account is taken of diminishing returns; a break-even analysis chart is necessary. Finally, the turnover objective is inadequate as an increase in turnover may not mean an increase in profit; cost restrictions need to be imposed.

LISTING DECISION AREAS AND ESTABLISHING INFORMATION NEEDS

Column (1) in the table of Management Information Analysis at the end of this section lists the main decision areas within the marketing department as might be deduced from objectives and interviews with managers. Existing reports, recorded policies, etc., are shown in Column (2) at the side of the relevant decision area. The analysis is confined to the information received and produced by the Marketing Director, Sales Manager and District Sales Supervisor. This restriction is imposed simply to keep the illustrative study within bounds. Ideally, the information system for the company as a whole should be tabulated.

Column (3) shows the originator of the report and Column (4) the destination. The frequency of reporting and the quantity received at the destination are shown in Columns (5) and (6),

In Column (7) are recorded the comments on the inadequacy, etc., of the existing information for the decision to be made. From such an analysis an ideal information system would be developed. In general, there is an absence of control information upon

(i)   the field sales force,
(ii) selling costs

    (a) uneconomic accounts,
    (b) uneconomic channels,
    (c) uneconomic products,
    (d) salesmen's expenses,

(iii) office efficiency,
(iv) advertising effectiveness and efficiency.

The existing 'control' information is also unstructured. Control reports should be structured for the various levels, though, if priorities demanded, all the reports would be available for higher management. As a minimum the Marketing Director would see all control reports once a year for his annual interview and appraisal of representatives.

Planning information is also inadequate in certain major decision areas, for example,

(i)   forecasting,
(ii) developing new products and locating market needs,
(iii) recruitment and training.

The market surveys received need to be analysed to draw out their implications for Strongwear. This is at present left to the Marketing Director. Such a busy executive is hardly likely to find time to carry out the sort of marketing analysis needed. It may be more profitable in a company of this size to set up a market analysis section to do this work and to commission other marketing surveys as the need arises.

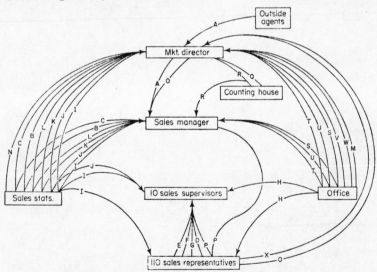

FIG. 35.—Existing documentary information flow within marketing department of Strongwear.   Identical forms are shown as having common roots.

Fig. 35 shows the existing information flow within the marketing department. All reports received and produced by the Marketing Director, Sales Manager and District Sales Supervisors are shown except for:

(i) information received by the Sales Manager from production departments about stock levels and proposed new products;

(ii) daily sales bulletin prepared by the Sales Manager and sent out to the field sales force and to all executives within marketing giving information on existing stock levels, and other information useful to field selling.

Fig. 35 points to a number of weaknesses:

(*a*) there is no exchange of reports between the Sales Manager and the District Sales Supervisors;

(*b*) information of a detailed nature is sent direct to the Marketing Director and by-passes the Sales Manager; information is even sent direct to the Marketing Director from the field sales force to which the Sales Manager and sales supervisors have no access.

MANAGEMENT INFORMATION ANALYSIS

Decision Area	Existing information pertinent to decision area	Originator	Destination	Frequency	Quantity	Comment
(1)	(2)	(3)	(4)	(5)	(6)	(7)
Marketing Decisions						
Selecting. Sales forecast	A. *Marketing Reports* Brand barometers for each product group.	Market Research Agency	Director	Every 3 mths.	30 per year	Inadequate basis for forecasting. Try: (a) correlation and ratio approaches; (b) time series analysis; (c) sales force composite method.
Distribution channels.	B. *Sales by Type of Outlet* Report showing sales by type of outlet viz: Dept. stores, men's outfitters, multiples, variety chain, mail order.	Territory admin. Manager	Director	Yearly	1	Changes mean little unless compared with national position. Compare with Board of Trade figures?

Decision Area	Existing information pertinent to decision area	Originator	Destination	Frequency	Quantity	Comment
	C. *Sales by Class of Outlet* Report showing sales by class of outlet, e.g. low-class or middle-class clientele.	Territory admin. Manager	Director & Sales Manager	Yearly	1	Report based on representative's assessment. Absence of uniformity. Use brand barometer data instead.
	D. *Customer Attitude Reports* Opinions given by customers to rep. entered on pre-printed form.	Representative	District Sales Supervisor	Weekly	10 per DSS per week	Substitute report from DSS to Sales Manager giving consensus of opinion of reps. as assessed at monthly meetings.
Price policy.	See Report A.					Implications for Strongwear *not* shown. Need for analysis. Market analysis section needed?
Sales territories.						Work Study investigation needed.
Sales territory potential.	See Report A.					Market analysis section needed?
Analysing market for each product.	See Report A.					Market analysis section needed?

M Advertising policy.	See Report A.	To determine message and media, information needed on: (a) Needs product satisfies — (1) use, (2) storage, (3) disposal; (b) Features that give competitive advantage; (c) Source of new business; (1) competitors, (2) new consumers, (3) other products, (4) more frequent use; (d) Existing level of awareness and preference for company's product. Inadequate. Research needed at point of sale.
Point of sales aids.	See Report A.	Goals need to be set based on information given above under Advertising.
Appraising advertising effectiveness.		
Developing new products and locating market needs.	See Report A.	Inadequate. More information needed. Product planning function necessary?
Staff Decisions Recruitment policy.		Need for job analysis.

Decision Area	Existing information pertinent to decision area	Originator	Destination	Frequency	Quantity	Comment
Work methods.						Need for investigation into alternative methods. Need for measurement.
Output standards.						
Quality standards.						Need for measurement.
Training programme.						Need for job analysis.
Performance appraisal.	E. *Copy Orders* Copies of orders received from customers.	Representative	District Sales Supervisor	Weekly	510 per week per DSS (i.e. about 50 per salesman)	Scrap: (a) Too many. (b) No standards for control to be exercised.
	F. *Representative's Line Sales by Value* Report shows sales made by rep. on each line. It summarizes copy orders which are attached.	Representative	District Sales Supervisor	Weekly	1	No standards to allow control. DSS complains that delay would result if information sent from Head Office. Delay O.K. as only preventive and not remedial action can be taken.
	G. *No Order Report* Memo recording reasons for failing to secure an order.	Representative	District Sales Supervisor	Weekly	10 per week per rep.	Scrap. DSS can examine customer records in detail if representative's performance is below standard.

Item	Office	District Sales Supervisor			Remarks
H. *Copy Letters* Copy of letters from Head Office to representatives.			Daily	24 per day per DSS	Scrap 10 out of 11 letters as these concerned with routine matters on orders.
I. *Direct and Personal Sales by Line by Quantity and Value* Returns showing sales by line for each salesman's area. No distinction is made between personal sales and orders received direct from customers, except in totals.	Territory Admin. Manager	(a) Rep. (b) DSS (c) Sales Manager (d) Director	Weekly	(a) Rep 1 (b) DSS11 (c) Sales Manager 110 (d) Director 110	There is a need for: (a) standards to allow control; (b) control information to be structured; (c) information to be shown also as moving annual total for planning purposes.
J. *Sales by Line for each DSS Area.* Return showing sales by line for each DSS area.	Territory Admin. Manager	(a) DSS (b) Sales Manager (c) Director	Weekly	DSS 1 Sales Manager 10 Director 10	As I above.
K. *Weekly Sales by Line all Territories* Return showing total sales by line.	Territory Admin. Manager	(a) Sales Manager (b) Director	Weekly	DSS 1 Director 1	As I above.

Decision Area	Existing information pertinent to decision area	Originator	Destination	Frequency	Quantity	Comment
	L. *Cumulative Sales by Line for all Territories* Return showing cumulative sales by line compared with previous year.	Territory Admin. Manager	(a) Sales Manager (b) Director	Weekly	DSS 1 Director 1	As I above.
	M. *Orders Received Report* Return showing number of orders received during the week as compared with corresponding week in previous year. The cumulative position is also shown.	Office	Director	Weekly	1	Scrap or compute average order value as indication of hand-to-mouth stocking.
	N. *Commission Return* Return showing details of commissions earned each month.	Territory Admin. Manager	Director	Monthly	1	Office should retain but be available on request.

O. *Representative's Call Cycle* Representative's plan for servicing his territory.	Representative	Director	When rep. appointed to territory	1 per month	Not to be sent to director. Office to check for completeness, i.e. no customers missed out, and DSS for effectiveness.
P. *Expenses Return* Pre-printed form on which representative records weekly expenses.	Representative	(a) DSS (b) Sales Manager	Weekly	DSS 11 per week. Sales Manager 121 per week.	No standards for control. Policy needed so administration could be carried out by office.
Remuneration policy.					Need for information on level of remuneration paid by competitors. Need to identify and analyse alternatives.
Cost Decisions Policy on expenses.					Need to define policy. Need to identify and analyse alternatives.
Budget preparation. Q. *Budget Comparison of Operating Costs.* Comparison of budgeted cost with actual cost for marketing dept. as a whole.	Accounts	Director	Monthly	1	Budget should give split between the various sections to allow sectional control.

Decision Area	Existing information pertinent to decision area	Originator	Destination	Frequency	Quantity	Comment
Cost analysis in field selling.						
(a) Uneconomic accounts.	R. *Doubtful Debt Return* List showing customers whose orders held up pending settlement of existing account.	Accounts	(a) Director (b) Sales Manager (c) Rep. (Section appropriate)	Weekly	Copy each	Representative alone to receive this information. Needs information to determine accounts whose business too small to justify representative calling. Time analysis needed.
(b) Uneconomic channels						Information needed on how representative apportions his time.
(c) Uneconomic products						Information needed on how representative apportions his time among the different products.
Decisions on Office Efficiency						
Office effectiveness	S. *Late Delivery Report* List showing details of orders delivered late.	Office	(a) Sales Manager (b) Director	Monthly	1 each	Trends should be plotted and management informed when outside acceptable limits.

	Prepared by	Sent to	Frequency	Copies	Notes
T. *Error Return* List giving details of errors made on orders—customer, nature of error and action taken.	Office	(a) Sales Manager (b) Director	Monthly	1 each	Trends should be plotted and management informed when outside acceptable limits.
U. *Report on Orders Cancelled* Return showing details of orders cancelled—nature customer and product.	Office	(a) Sales Manager (b) Director	Monthly	1 each	Trends should be plotted and management informed when outside acceptable limits.
V. *Staff Return* Return showing details of staff leaving or joining office.	Office	Director	Monthly	1 each	No need to send to director. Labour turnover figure can be included in annual report.
W. *Letters and Enquiries Return* Shows: (a) number of letters received re orders as compared with previous years.	Office Manager	Sales Manager	Weekly		(a) Scrap.

Decision Area	Existing information pertinent to decision area	Originator	Destination	Frequency	Quantity	Comment
	(b) Number of public and trade enquiries re products as compared with previous years. The enquiries are classified by line.	Office Manager	Sales Manager	Weekly		(b) May be useful to advertising.
Cost						Need for procedures analysis and work measurement programme.

DESIGNING COMMUNICATION CHANNELS FOR
THE INFORMATION FLOW, AND GROUPING DECISION
AREAS TO MINIMIZE COMMUNICATIONS BURDEN

The decision schedule can be useful in organization work. The schedule shown (Appendix II) is for field sales force and the main marketing decisions. Such a schedule can first be completed to indicate the existing allocation of decision-making authority together with the appropriate communication networks, that is to say the input to the decision-maker and the output from the decision-maker to those to be informed after a decision is made. The schedule can be examined to reduce the communications burden by:

(i)   grouping together decision-makers whose work is most inter-dependent; where a person receives or produces information for some decision-maker more than he receives or produces information for any other decision-maker, there may be a case for grouping the two together;
(ii) re-allocating decision-making authority;
(iii) changing the source or distribution of information.

An examination of decision schedules for Strongwear as a whole might suggest a number of organizational changes in the marketing department to improve decision-making and co-ordination. A revised grouping might be that shown in the chart below.

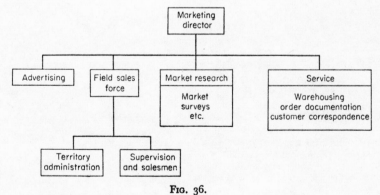

Fig. 36.

A market research section would probably be justified by the level of business undertaken, though the actual fieldwork may still be undertaken by outside agents. Without more marketing analysis, company decision-making would be merely speculative.

The territory administration section might be better grouped under the Sales Manager to achieve better co-ordination, as the work of the Sales Manager and the territory administration section are closely interwoven. Finally, the bulk of decisions concerned with customer service may be grouped together. At present, customer correspondence and order documentation come under the Marketing Director but not warehousing and despatch. Such a suggested grouping could only be recommended after examining other decision schedules completed for the company as a whole since a grouping for service may be in conflict with other goals.

DECISION SCHEDULE

Box Abbreviations

AD = Advertising Manager
DSS = District Sales Supervisor
MD = Marketing Director
MR = Market Research Manager
OAD = Office Administration Head
PM = Personnel Manager
SF = Sales Force
SM = Sales Manager
TAD = Territory Administration Head

Column Abbreviations

A = Non-Supervisory Level
B = Supervisory Level
C = Manager

DECISION AREA	Makes Recommendations			To be informed after Decision Made			Information Source — Direct Aims Ways and Means			Direct Aims Only			Advisory Only			Makes Decision — Except in Exceptional Cases			Exceptional Cases			Appropriate Information
	A	B	C	A	B	C	A	B	C	A	B	C	A	B	C	A	B	C	A	B	C	Reports, etc.
Staff Recruitment																						
Policy	DSS	DSS		PM SM DSS	SM								PM SM	SM		MD	MD	MD				Job Analysis
Procedure					MD SF OAD								SM			PM	SM	MD	SM	MD		Personnel Procedure Manual
Selection				MD PM									PM DSS			SM	SM	MD		MD		Job Analysis
Staff increase within policy limits				PM MD									DSS			SM	SM	MD		MD		Field Analysis (Work Study)
Work Methods																						
Methods	MR AD SF	MR AD DSS	SM	SF DSS		SM				SM	MD		MR DSS	MR DSS		DSS	SM	MD		MD		Work study and O.R. survey
Output	SF	DSS		SF DSS	DSS	SM				MD	MD		DSS MR	MR		SM	SM	MD				Sales Budget
Quality	SF	DSS		SF DSS	DSS	SM				MD	MD		MR DSS	DSS		SM	SM	MD				Merit Rating Scheme
Staff Training																						
Training Programme	DSS	DSS		MD PM	DSS MD					MD	MD		PM OSS MR	PM OSS		SM	SM	MD	MD	MD		Job analysis
Staff Motivation and Control																						
Performance appraisal	SF DSS	DSS	SM	SF DSS	DSS	SM							TA			SM DSS	SM MD	MD	MD	MD		Relative performance on quota

Table (printed sideways on the page). Columns are five groups of A / B / C authority columns plus a "Reports, etc" column.

	A	B	C	A	B	C	A	B	C	A	B	C	A	B	C	Reports, etc
Staff Remuneration and Expenses																
Starting wage	DSS			PM			MD			SM	MD	MD	MD			Job evaluation and salary policy
Wage increase	DSS, SF	DSS	SM					Board		SM	MD	MD				Board policy
Overtime	DSS, SF	DSS, SM	SM					Board								
Travel expenses up to specified limit	SF, DSS	DSS		TA	TA	MD	SM			SM	SM	SM	DSS	MD	MD	Expenses (policy) Scheme
Entertainment specified up to limit	SF, DSS	DSS		TA	TA	MD	SM			SM	SM	SM	DSS	MD	MD	Expenses (policy) scheme
Staff Promotion and Transfer																
Promotion within Dept.	SF	DSS		DSS						SM	MD	MD	MD			Performance reports
Transfer within Dept.	SF	DSS		DSS						SM	MD	MD	MD			Market reports
Staff Dismissal	PM, DSS			DSS			SM			MD, SM	MD, SM	Board	DSS			Reports on performance and conduct
Staff Absences																
Annual Holiday				MR	MR					DSS	SM	MD	SM	MD		Peaks and troughs in work flow (i.e. seasonal business fluctuations)

	Makes Recommendations A	B	C	To be informed after Decision Made A	B	C	Info Source: Direct Aims Ways and Means A	B	C	Info Source: Direct Aims Only A	B	C	Info Source: Advisory Only A	B	C	Makes Decision: Except in Exceptional Cases A	B	C	Makes Decision: Exceptional Cases A	B	C	Appropriate Information: Reports etc.
Staff Communication																							
Interpreting policies to subordinates	PM	PM	PM	Subordinates						MD	MD					DSS	SM	MD	SM	MD		Sales Bulletins
Staff Organization																							
Allocating work				SF DSS	DSS	SM							MR TA AD	MR TA AD		DSS	SM	MD	SM	MD		Co-ord. committee meeting
Grouping work																SM	SM	MD	MD			Work study and O.R. Survey
Marketing								DEPARTMENTAL	DECISIONS													
Sales Budget	All in Marketing			All cost Centres									M.R. & production			Board						Sales Forecast
Market requirements	SF DSS			Product planning Committee							MD		MR			MR						Market Surveys
Channels of distribution													MR SM			MD				SM		Market surveys
Price policy				Marketing and production									MR & costing			Board						Cost analysis and market surveys
Discount policy				Marketing and production									MR & costing			Board						Cost analysis and market surveys
Credit Policy				Field sales force & accounts									MD			Accounting Director						Analysis of alternative credit policies

Activity			Comptroller	Accounting	Accounts		Information required
Customer credit				TA, MR	SM, DSS		'Bradsheet' & customer record card
Sales territories		SF		MR	SM, DSS	MD	Work load analysis
Territory Potential	DSS	SF		AD, SM	MR	MD	Market surveys
Market surveys within budget		MD			MR	MD	Analysis of past usefulness
Analysing market for…		MD, AD, SM	MD				
Advertising policy	MR	MD, MR, SM	MD	MR	AD	MD	Analysis of alternative advertising policies
Point of sales aids	SF, DSS	SF, DSS, MD	MR	MR	AD, SM	MD	Analysis of alternative point of sales aids
Determining effectiveness		MD			MR, AD	MD	Market consumer attitude surveys
Financial							
Preparing cost budgets		Each section head	Comptroller	Accounting	Each section Head	MD	Sales budget
Determine actual cost budgets				Comptroller	MD	Board	Sales budget
Analysis of clerical procedures			MD		O & M		
Distribution cost analysis			MD		Cost accountant		

REFERENCES

1. CHAMBERLAIN, N. W., *The Firm—Micro Economic Planning & Action*, McGraw-Hill, London & New York, 1962.
2. SOLOMON, EZRA, *The Theory of Financial Management*, Columbia University Press, New York, 1963.
3. MORRIS, W. T., *Management Science in Action*, Richard D. Irwin, Homewood Ill., 1962.
4. First International Seminar on Marketing Management, Indiana University, February 1961, *Business Horizons*, Indiana University.
5. DRUCKER, P. F., *The Practice of Management*, Heinemann, London, 1955.
6. HALL, A. D., *A Methodology for Systems Engineering*, Van Nostrand, Princeton, 1962.
7. *Business Week*, November 19th, 1955.
8. BATTERSBY, A., *Network Analysis*, Macmillan, London, 1963.
9. RICE, A. K., *The Enterprise and its Environment: A System Theory of Management Organisation*, p. 183, Tavistock Publications, London, 1963.
10. URWICK, L., *The Elements of Administration*, p. 18, Pitman, London, 1943.
11. *Ibid.* p. 26.
12. FAYOL, H., *General & Industrial Management*, p. 43, Pitman, London, 1949.
13. *Ibid.* p. 53.
14. URWICK, *The Elements of Administration*, p. 42.
15. SIMON, H. A., *Administrative Behaviour*, p. 112, Macmillan, New York, 1957.
16. URWICK, L., 'Axioms of Organisation', *Public Administration Magazine* (London), October, 1935, p. 348.
17. GULICK, L., and L. URWICK (Eds), *Papers on the Science of Administration*, paper by V. A. Graicunas, "Relationship and Organisation", Institute of Public Administration, New York, 1937.
18. DAVIS, R. C., *The Influence of the Unit of Supervision and the Span of Executive Control on the Economy of Organisation Structure*, Bureau of Research Monograph No. 26, Ohio State University, 1941.
19. SIMON, H. A., 'The Span of Control: A Reply', *Advanced Management*, April 1957.
20. HAIRE, M. (ed.), *Modern Organisation Theory*, John Wiley, London and New York, 1961.
21. SUOJANEN, W. W., 'The Span of Control—Fact or Fable', *Advanced Management* November 1955.
22. COPEMAN, G., *How the Executive Spends His Time*, Business Publications, London, 1963.
23. CARLSON, S., *Executive Behaviour*, Stromberg, Stockholm, 1951.
24. FULLER, D., *Organising, Planning & Scheduling for Engineering Operations*, Industrial Education Institute, 1962.
25. ROBBINS COMMITTEE, *Higher Education Report*, para. 765, Cmnd. 2154, H.M.S.O., London, 1963.
26. CLARK, J. M., *Studies in the Economics of Overhead Cost*, University of Chicago Press, 1923.
27. ROBINSON, E. A. G., *The Structure of Competitive Industry*, Cambridge University Press, 1935.

28. FOLLETT, M. P., 'The Illusion of Final Authority', *Advanced Management*, September 1963.
29. FAYOL, *General & Industrial Management*, p. 25.
30. DUBIN, R. (ed.), *Human Relations in Administration*, p. 75., Prentice-Hall, Englewood Cliffs N.J., 1961.
31. SIMON, *Administrative Behaviour*, p. 20.
32. MORRIS, *Management Science in Action*, p. 67.
33. ROBINSON, *The Structure of Competitive Industry*, p. 47.
34. FAYOL, *General & Industrial Management*, p. 21.
35. STIEGLITZ, H., 'Organisation Planning', *B.I.M. Digest*, 1964.
36. KOONTZ, H. & C. O'DONNELL, *Principles of Management*, p. 93, McGraw-Hill, New York, 1959.
37. HAIRE, M. (ed.), *Organisation Theory in Industrial Practice*, p. 3, John Wiley, London & New York, 1962.
38. ALLEN, L. A., *Management & Organisation*, McGraw-Hill, New York, 1959.
39. Anbar Monograph No. I, Anbar Publications Ltd., London, 1963.
40. FAYOL, *General & Industrial Management*, p. 21.
41. KOONTZ & O'DONNELL, *Principles of Management*.
42. BRECH, E. F. L., *Organization: the Framework of Management*, p. 58, Longmans, London, 1957.
43. BENNET, C. L., *The A.M.A. Manual of Position Guides*, p. 126, American Management Association, New York, 1958.
44. PFIFFNER, J. M. & F. P. SHERWOOD, *Administrative Organisation*, p. 218, Prentice-Hall, Englewood Cliffs, N.J., 1960.
45. BENNET, *The A.M.A. Manual of Position Guides*, p. 121.
46. SCHLESINGER, A. M., *The Coming of the New Deal*, p. 528 Houghton Mifflin, Boston, 1959.
47. DRUCKER, *The Practice of Management*.
48. URWICK, *The Elements of Administration*, p. 47.
49. HAIRE, *Organisation Theory in Industrial Practice*, p. 5.
50. URWICK, *The Elements of Administration*, p. 48.
51. ROBINSON, *The Structure of Competitive Industry*.
52. CAIRNCROSS, A., *Introduction to Economics*, 3rd edition, p. 91, Butterworth, London, 1960.
53. ROBINSON, *The Structure of Competitive Industry*, p. 43.
54. URWICK, *The Elements of Administration*, p. 32.
55. *Ibid.* p. 32.
56. GERTH, H. H. & C. WRIGHT MILLS., *From Max Weber: Essays in Sociology*, Oxford University Press, 1946.
57. URWICK, L. & E. F. L. BRECH., *The Making of Scientific Management*, Vol. III The Hawthorne Investigations, p. ix. Pitman, 1947.
58. MAIER, NORMAN R. F., *Psychology in Industry*, Houghton Mifflin, Boston, 1960.
59. ARGYRIS, C., *Personality and Organisation*, Harper and Row, New York, 1957.
60. MCGREGOR, D., *The Human Side of Enterprise*, McGraw-Hill, London & New York, 1960.
61. ROETHLISBERGER, F. J. & W. J. DICKSON, *Management & the Worker*, Harvard University Press, Cambridge Mass., 1939.
62. VITELES, M. S., *Motivation & Morale in Industry*, p. 193, Staples Press, 1953.
63. *Ibid.* p. 205.
64. *Ibid.* p. 180.
65. MACCOBY, E. E., T. M. NEWCOMB, E. L. HARTLEY (eds.), *Readings in Social Psychology*, p. 174, Holt Rinehart & Winston, New York, 1947.
66. WHYTE, W. H., *The Organization Man*, Jonathan Cape, London, 1957.
67. REISMAN, D., *The Lonely Crowd*, Yale University Press, New Haven, 1960.

68. SHERIF, M., 'An Experimental Study of Stereotypes', *Journal of Abnormal & Social Psychology*, 1935, pp. 29 & 371-375.
69. VITELES, *Motivation & Morale in Industry*, p. 229.
70. SELLTIZ, C., M. JAHODA, M. DEUTSCH., & S. W. COOK, *Research Methods in Social Relations*, p. 311, Methuen, London, 1962.
71. HEMPHILL, J. K. & C. M. WESTIE, 'The Measurement of Group Dimensions', *Journal of Psychology*, 1950, pp. 29 & 325-342.
72. LIKERT, R., *New Patterns of Management*, McGraw-Hill, London & New York, 1961.
73. GAGNE, R. M., & E. A. FLEISHMAN, *Psychology and Human Performance*, p. 322, Holt Rinehart & Winston, New York, 1959.
74. LIPPITT, R. & R. K. WHITE, *Autocracy and Democracy: An Experimental Inquiry*, Harper and Row, New York, 1960.
75. VITELES, *Motivation & Morale in Industry*, p. 149.
76. LIKERT, *New Patterns of Management*, p. 68.
77. MACCOBY, NEWCOMB & HARTLEY (eds.), *Readings in Social Psychology*.
78. VITELES, *Motivation & Morale in Industry*, p. 168.
79. ARGYRIS, C., *Interpersonal Competence and Organisational Effectiveness*, p. 135, Dorsey Press, Homewood Ill., 1962.
80. LEAVITT, H. J. (ed.), *The Social Science of Organisations*, p. 62, Prentice-Hall, Englewood Cliffs, N. J., 1963.
81. MCGREGOR, *The Human Side of Enterprise*.
82. HABERSTROH, C. J. & A. H. RUBINSTEIN, *Some Theories of Organisation*, p. 178, Dorsey Press & Richard Irwin, Homewood Ill., 1960.
83. *Ibid.* p. 184.
84. *Ibid.* p. 179.
85. WHYTE, W. F., *Human Relations in the Restaurant Industry*, McGraw-Hill, New York, 1948.
86. SHERIF, M., 'Superordinate Goals in the Reduction of Intergroup Conflict', *American Journal of Sociology*, Vol. 63, No. 4, 1958.
87. DRUCKER, *The Practice of Management*, p. 177.
88. GANGE & FLEISHMAN, *Psychology and Human Performance*, p. 313.
89. LIKERT, *New Patterns of Management*.
90. HAIRE, *Modern Organisation Theory*, p. 250.
91. DUBIN, *Human Relations in Administration*, p. 347.
92. SIMON, *Administrative Behaviour*.
93. BROWN, W., *Exploration in Management*, p. 231, Heinemann, London, 1960.
94. STROTHER, G. (ed.), *Social Science Approaches to Business Behaviour*, p. 169, Tavistock Publications, London, 1962.
95. BROWN, *Exploration in Management*, p. 136.
96. STROTHER, *Social Science Approaches to Business Behaviour*, p. 180.
97. BROWN, *Exploration in Management*, p. 98.
98. FAYOL, *General & Industrial Management*, p. 21.
99. BROWN, *Exploration in Management*, p. 55.
100. DUBIN, *Human Relations in Administration*, p. 72.
101. DRUCKER, *The Practice of Management*, p. 227.
102. TRIST, E. L., G. W. HIGGIN, H. MURRAY, & A. B. POLLOCK, *Organisational Choice: Capabilities of Groups at the Coal Face Under Changing Technologies*, Tavistock Publications, London, 1962.
103. STEBBING, L. S., *Philosophy and the Physicists*, pp. 168-9, Dover, New York, 1958.
104. SIMON, *Administrative Behaviour*, p. 4.
105. KNIGHT, F. H., *Risk, Uncertainty and Profit*, Houghton Mifflin, Boston, 1921.
106. SIMON, H. A., *The Science of Management Decision*, Harper and Row, New York, 1960.

107. ASHBY, W. ROSS, *Design for a Brain*, Chapman & Hall, London, 1954.
108. GALBRAITH, J. K., *The Affluent Society*, p. 101, Houghton Mifflin, Boston, Hamish Hamilton, London, 1958.
109. MEYER, J. R. & E. KUH, *The Investment Decision: An Empirical Study*, Harvard University Press, Cambridge Mass., 1957.
110. VAN NEUMANN, J. & O. MORGENSTERN, *Theory of Games and Economic Behaviour*, 2nd Edition, Princeton University Press, Princeton N. J., 1947.
111. CHAMBERLAIN, *The Firm—Micro Economic Planning & Action*, p. 395.
112. VILLIERS, R., *Dynamic Management in Industry*, Prentice-Hall, Englewood Cliffs, N.J., 1960.
113. *D.O.D. & N.A.S.A. Guide to PERT/Cost*, U.S. Government Printing Office, Washington, 1962.
114. ANDERSON, SAUNDERS and WEEKS, *Business Reports*, McGraw-Hill, New York, 1957.
115. SHANNON, C. & W. WEAVER, *Mathematical Theory of Communication*, p. 98, The University of Illinois Press, Urbana Ill., 1949.
116. *Ibid.* p. 95.
117. *Ibid.* p. 97.
118. *Ibid.* p. 98.
119. HICK, W. E., 'On the Rate of Gain of Information', *Quarterly Journal of Experimental Psychology*, Part I, February 1952.
120. LEE, W. M., 'Some aspects of a Control and Communication System', *Operational Research Quarterly*, Vol. 10, No. 4, 1959.
121. ACKOFF, R. L., *Management Science*, April 1958.
122. SPROTT, W. J. H., *Human Groups*, Pelican Books, London, 1958.
123. ROWE, A. J., *Management International*, 1962/2, p. 20.
124. FORRESTER, J. W., *Industrial Dynamics*, John Wiley, New York, 1961.
125. RICE, A. K., *The Enterprise and its Environment: A System Theory of Management Organisation*, Tavistock Publication, London, 1963.
126. BATTERSBY, A., *Network Analysis*.
127. ROWE, A. J., *Management International*, 1962/2, p. 21.
128. SIMON, *Administrative Behaviour*, p. 154.
129. BROWN, *Exploration in Management*.
130. SIMON, *The New Science of Management Decision*, p. 39.

Advertising, Goals, 22-23.
Allen, L. A., 26, 29, 53, 56, 57.
American Management Association (A.M.A.), 34, 58, 59.
Argyris, C., 43, 75, 99.
Asch, S. E., 82.
Attitudes, 84-88.
Authority, Delegation of, 50-55, 111-114, 155-158.

Barnard, C., 111.
Bavelas, A., 98, 146.
Bennett, C. L., 58.
Brech, E. F. L., 26, 58, 64, 72.
Brown, W., 112, 114, 115, 117, 159-160.

Cairncross, A., 68.
Carlson, S., 36.
Certainty (and Decision making), 131-132.
Chain of Command, 14, 62.
Chamberlain, N. W., 18, 138, 139.
Clark, J. M., 39.
Committees, 49, 108.
Communication, 116, 143-148, 151-158.
Control, 136-142.
Co-ordination, 41-45, 47, 52, 56.
 Co-ordination & Committees, 49.
 Co-ordination & Divisionalisation, 50.

Davis, R. C., 32, 33.
Decentralisation, 55-57.
Decision making, 127-135.
Dickson, W. J., 79.
Divisionalization, 50, 55.
Drucker, P., 64, 104, 121-122.
Dubin, R., 108.

Economies of Scale, Grouping for, 39-41.
Efficiency: Definition, 21.
Employee centred, 91-92.
Ergonomics, 125, 160.

Fayol, H., 26, 27, 28, 30, 42, 53, 57, 116.

Feedback, 137-138.
Fleishman, E. A., 92.
Follett, M. P., 41.
Frustration, 75-77.
Functional Relationship, 64, 65.

Galbraith, J. K., 132.
Goals (see Objectives).
Graicunas, V. A., 31-32.
Group dynamics, 97-108.

Haire, M., 34, 53-55, 66, 113-115.
Harwood manufacturing, 97-99, 118.
Hawthorne experiment, 77-80, 85, 87.

Information, 135-143.
Innovation (product), 21.

Job-centred (supervision), 91.
Job enlargement, 121-124.

'Key' Departments, 29.
 Activities, 30, 45.
Knight, F. H., 131.
Koestler, Arthur, 81.
Koontz, H., 53, 57.

Lateral relationship, 66.
Leadership, 83, 93-95.
Leavitt, H. J., 146.
Lewin, K., 97.
Line (relationship), 62.
Link-pin theory, 107-109.
Likert, R., 91-92, 95, 96, 108.
Lippitt, R., 94-95.

Maier, N. R. F., 75.
Majority effect, 82.
Managerial position description (see Schedule of Responsibilities).
Marketing: as Objective, 20-21.
Massarik, F., 109.
Mayo, E., 72.
McGregor, D., 75, 100, 101.
Morale, 86, 94.
Morris, W. T., 43.
Motives, 74, 75, 84.

Noise, 144.

Objectives, 14-25, 128, 129.
O'Donnell, C., 53, 57.
Operational Research, 130.
Organization definition, 13.
    Approaches to, 14.
    Deficiencies in, 13.
    Flat versus pyramidal, 102-106.
    'Matrix' type, 153.

Participation, 92-100, 109-111.
Personal assistant, 65.
Planning, 136.
Policy, 24-25, 132.
Position descriptions (see Schedules of responsibility).
Principles of organization, 43.
Problem solving, 83.
Profit: as Primary objective, 18-19.
Project management, 151-154.

Redundancy, 144.
Responsibility, 57-62, 114-119, 158-160.
Rice, A. K., 27, 86, 149, 150.
Riesman, D., 82-83.
Risk, 131.
Robbins Report, 39, 45-47.
Robinson, E. A. G., 39, 48, 49, 68.
Roethlisberger, F. J., 79, 117.
Role, 119-120.
Rowe, A. J., 134, 147, 154, 155.

Schedules of responsibility, 58-62.
Selekman, B. M., 82.
Shannon, C., 145.
Sherif, M., 102.
Simon, H. A., 28, 33, 43, 111-113, 130, 134, 155, 161.
Smith, Adam, 67.
Sociogram, 89, 106, 107.

Span of control, 29-37.
Specialization individual, 67-71, 121-124.
    Sectional, 106.
Standards, 117, 118, 119, 136-141.
Status, 119-120.
Stebbing, Susan, 126.
Strauss, G., 100.
Suojanen, W. W., 34, 36.
Supervisor: behaviour, 90-101.
Systems, 125-128.
    Open and closed loop systems, 137-138.

Tannenbaum, R., 109.
Taylor, F. W., 26, 53, 67.
Theory, 'X' & 'Y', 100-101.
Trist, E. L., 122, 123.

Uncertainty (and decision-making), 131-132.
Unity of direction principle, 42-44.
Unity of command principle, 62, 63, 64.
Urwick, L., 26, 27, 28, 30, 53, 66, 67, 68, 69, 71, 72.

Villiers, R., 141.
Viteles, M. S., 79, 86.

Weaver, W., 144.
Weber, M., 72.
White, R. K., 94, 95.
Whyte, W. F., 101.
Whyte, W. H., 82.
Work groups, 77-84.
    Measuring group dimensions, 88.
    Inter-group behaviour, 101, 102.
    Work group authority, 113-114.
Work load on management, 35-39.
Work organization, 67-71, 120-124, 160-161.

GEORGE ALLEN & UNWIN LTD

Head Office
40 Museum Street, London W.C.1
Telephone: 01-405 8577

Sales, Distribution and Accounts Departments
Park Lane, Hemel Hempstead, Herts.
Telephone: 0442 3244

Argentina: Rodriguez Pena 1653-118, Buenos Aires
Australia: Cnr. Bridge Road and Jersey Street, Hornsby, N.S.W. 2077
Canada: 2330 Midland Avenue, Agincourt, Ontario
Greece: 7 Stadiou Street, Athens 125
India: 103/5 Fort Street, Bombay 1
2850 Bepin Behari Ganguli Street, Calcutta 12
2/18 Mount Road, Madras 2
4/21-22B Asaf Ali Road, New Delhi 1
Japan: 29/13 Hongo 5 Chome, Bunkyo, Tokyo 113
Kenya: P.O. Box 30583, Nairobi
Lebanon: Deeb Building, Jeanne d'Arc Street, Beirut
Mexico: Serapio Rendon 125, Mexico 4, D.F.
New Zealand: 46 Lake Road, Northcote, Auckland 9
Nigeria: P.O. Box 62, Ibadan
Pakistan: Karachi Chambers, McLeod Road, Karachi 2
22 Falettis' Hotel, Egerton Road, Lahore
Philippines: 3 Malaming Street, U.P. Village, Quezon City, D-505
Singapore: 248c/1 Orchard Road, Singapore 9
South Africa: P.O. Box 23134, Joubert Park, Johannesburg
West Indies: Rockley New Road, St. Lawrence 4, Barbados